TWO
SISTERS
AND
A PIANO
AND OTHER PLAYS

Other books by Nilo Cruz available from TCG

ANNA IN THE TROPICS

ANA EN EL TRÓPICO
(Spanish Translation)

BEAUTY OF THE FATHER

Two Sisters and a Piano

and Other Plays

Nilo Cruz

THEATRE COMMUNICATIONS GROUP
NEW YORK
2007

This publication is made possible in part with public funds from
the New York State Council on the Arts, a State Agency.

TCG books are exclusively distributed to the book trade by Consortium
Book Sales and Distribution, 1045 Westgate Dr., St. Paul, MN 55114.

LIBRARY OF CONGRESS CATALOGING-IN-PUBLICATION DATA
Cruz, Nilo.
Two sisters and a piano and other plays / Nilo Cruz. — 1st ed.
p. cm.
ISBN-13: 978-1-55936-258-0
ISBN-10: 1-55936-258-8
I. Title.
PS3603.R895T962 2006
812'.6—dc22
2006031005

Book design and composition by Lisa Govan
Cover design by Pentagram
Cover photograph by Michal Daniel of Daphne Rubin-Vega (Sophia, left) and
Adriana Sevan (María Celia) from The Public Theater production
Author photograph by Oskar Landi

First Edition, November 2007

CONTENTS

INTRODUCTION

By Janice Paran

I've known Nilo Cruz since 1994, when he was commissioned to write a one-act for a festival of new work at the McCarter Theatre, where I was the resident dramaturg. He was one of a dozen or so writers invited to riff on the idea of "home," and his short play, a monologue called *Madrigal*, stopped me in my tracks.

I don't remember anymore whether the play's setting was specifically identified, but even on the page its sense of place was palpable. Cuba—Nilo's Cuba, which is part myth, part memory—was its inspiration, its currency, its aroma, its refrain. With a few atmospheric strokes, he conjured up a furtive, languid and mesmerizing world whose local colors were new to me, but whose intimacy, vibrancy and voluptuousness beckoned further acquaintance. With the McCarter's artistic staff trying hard not to breathe down his neck, he quickly expanded the piece into a full-length play, *A Park in Our House*, which became the centerpiece of our festival and led to several subsequent projects.

What first attracted me to Nilo's work still attracts me: its psychic richness and alluring theatricality. He has an instinct for stories and characters that not only suit the stage but in fact require its dependence on everything language *doesn't* provide: the silences between and beneath words, kinetic currents, the almost physical pressure of onstage time and the fragile compact with a live audience. Jean Cocteau famously made the distinction between poetry *in* the theatre and poetry *of* the theatre, and though Nilo has often been credited with the former, his deeper accomplishment is that he understands and strives to create the latter.

Dreaming in Cuban, the name of a novel by Cristina Garcia, could serve as a description of his aesthetic. Born in Cuba to a shoe salesman and a seamstress, Nilo was just shy of ten when his family, frustrated by the growing militancy of the Castro regime, left in 1970 aboard a Freedom Flight bound for Miami; a ninety-mile hop to a different universe. With this sudden cultural shift, it is not surprising that his storytelling, through a kind of intuitive personal alchemy, imparts a cross-cultural vigor that reflects his experience of the world, and though he writes in English, the rhythms, colors and inflections of Spanish dance beneath the surface of his texts. He has frequently (though not exclusively, as this volume demonstrates) looked to his homeland for inspiration, mining its history, its culture and his own recollections in a continuing effort to fix, for a moment, some details of its confounding realities. But all of his plays, regardless of provenance, chart deeply moving landscapes of longing, loss and the will to survive.

His voice is poignant, humorous, humane, often extravagant and always disarming. Elements of romance, fantasy and surreal invention brush the lives of his characters, men and women (children, too, sometimes) of courage and contrariness, doggedly pursuing their dreams or passionately refashioning their circumstances with all the resources they can muster. They are at the heart of his beguiling dramaturgy. He has been labeled a magic realist, a phrase too readily applied to Latino writers, but one that acknowledges the role that wonder plays in his imagination and the fact that emotional realities, as he depicts them, sometimes require larger-than-life means of expression.

If Nilo has yet to enter the theatrical mainstream (although *Anna in the Tropics*, his 2003 Pulitzer Prize–winning play, seen at numerous regional theatres and on Broadway, moved him closer to that benchmark), he has been quietly assembling a devoted following in not-for-profit institutions around the country. His work has been developed and produced at Arena Stage, Florida Stage, San Francisco's Magic Theatre, the McCarter Theatre, Florida's New Theatre in Coral Gables, New York Theatre Workshop, the Oregon Shakespeare Festival, New York's Public Theater, California's South Coast Repertory and Seattle Repertory Theatre, among others. Artistic directors who have worked with him tend to invite him back, charmed by his gentle ways, energized by the originality of his theatrical vision and bewitched by his sensuous stage poetry. They're also increasingly aware of the difference his sensibility has made to a theatrical repertoire that is not yet as diverse as the nation it purports to reflect.

Two Sisters and a Piano, originally written as a radio play and expanded for the stage, is the story of two women, both artists, living under house arrest in Cuba in 1991 just as the collapse of the Soviet Union seems to promise new ways of thinking about old orthodoxies. It is Nilo's most political play, which is only to say that politics increase the barometric pressure in the drama, not that they take center stage—a proposition that holds no attraction for him.

María Celia and her sister, Sofia, once the toast of a circle of artists and intellectuals, have recently been released from prison (their punishment for having signed a manifesto in support of Perestroika, an offense borrowed from the real-world experiences of Cuban writer María Elena Cruz Varela). With only each other and their memories for company, they stave off boredom and despair with spirit, industry and somewhat overactive imaginations. Each has her private retreat—for María Celia, it's the rooftop where she recites letters to an absent husband, and for Sofia, it's the rundown piano, a family heirloom, where she can indulge her passion for Lecuona and other "counterrevolutionary" composers. When those don't suffice, the sisters share the guilty pleasure of eavesdropping on the man next door, whose escapades, erotic and otherwise, they invent for their amusement.

They also share an increasing urge to live dangerously, as does Lieutenant Portuondo, the government official assigned to their case. Dedicated to the revolutionary ideals of the regime he serves, he is nonetheless a closeted fan of María Celia's writing, a confession that opens a fissure between the ideology he professes and the promptings of his inner life. As his visits to the sisters become more frequent, and his interest in María Celia begins to complicate the delicate balance of power the three of them have negotiated within their hothouse, impulse trumps caution, with predictably calamitous results.

Yet it's impossible to draw a line separating the victims from the oppressors in the play, impossible for Nilo to argue Cuban politics on an ideological plane. He is temperamentally a romantic, partial to the lovers, loners and artists who populate his plays and chafe against the bonds of social custom, law or prejudice. All of the characters in *Two Sisters and a Piano* are marooned, forsaken by a revolution that served some needs but neglected others; all long for beauty in a culture that sanctions utility. The island has forgotten, says María Celia, "that there are revolutions within revolutions." Theirs is a secondhand existence, one marked by waiting and watching and listening, by an enforced passivity that is counter to their natures. And while they manage, for a time, to slip their fetters, the world they live in reasserts its authority with a quiet vengeance.

Waiting may be Cuba's national malady, but it can also be a form of fighting, according to the title character in *Hortensia and the Museum of Dreams*. Set in 1998 during Pope John Paul II's historic visit to Cuba, an event which, depending on your point of view, demonstrated either a softening of the Cuban government's stance on religious expression or its knack for public relations, the play hopscotches between two tales: one of a brother and sister facing the prospect of a reunion decades after a Pedro Pan humanitarian flight transported them from their Cuban childhood to an American future, and one of an Afro-Cuban diva who maintains a mom-and-pop reliquary called The Museum of Dreams. The link between the two stories is Luciana, the transplanted sister—now an American journalist—who has returned to Cuba to cover the papal visit, despite her trepidations about seeing her brother, Luca, whose own visit coincides with hers. After catching a glimpse of him in Havana shortly after their arrival, an incident that unsettles her for reasons that can soon be guessed at, Luciana sets off for the countryside, a detour which takes up much of the action of the play but proves to be the most direct route to her real homecoming.

Once out of the city, she finds herself unexpectedly on the doorstep of Hortensia, a secondary character vying for the lead, one of Nilo's most satisfying and exuberant stage creations. Part politician, part priestess, she is a one-woman curator of Cuba's everyday miracles, an under-the-radar faith healer. People all over the island send her their testimonials (a statue that turned into a goldfish, a saint that appeared in the laundry) scribbled on scraps of paper, and she lovingly files them and displays the ribbons, rosaries and retablos that accompany them. Her take-no-prisoners efforts to recruit Luciana to her cause—which is nothing less than an audience with the pope so that her rag-tag collection can be elevated to a national institution—is as self-serving as it is big-hearted.

It's also a welcome diversion for Luciana, whose long-lost brother tugs at her consciousness with sly persistence. He is the past she cannot outrun, and hints of the transgressive intimacy they shared as children—mirrored in the bond between Hortensia's grown sons, more boys than men in demeanor and sophistication—defy easy categorization. Torn from their moorings and dispatched to a neverland as seductive and subversive as anything J. M. Barrie imagined, Luciana and Luca lost their childhood, and in doing so, found each other. Their necessary but impossible love—a frequent Nilo theme—limns the difference between innocence and naïveté. When Hortensia, having decided that the museum's time hasn't come, sends the younger woman off in search of her brother, Luciana has learned enough about miracles to recognize the one that's waiting for her.

For the protagonists in *A Bicycle Country*, Cuba is not a place of reckoning but quite literally a point of departure. Inspired by the *balseros*, the Cuban rafters whose desperate efforts to reach the United States aboard jerry-built vessels made headlines in the 1990s, the play is divided into two parts whose titles—"Tierra" and "Agua"—frame the elemental nature of the narrative. The first part, spanning a period of six months in the lives of Julio, an invalid; his friend, Pepe; and his nurse, Ines, is a warm-up for what's to come.

Ines is initially the outsider, reluctantly putting Julio through his convalescent paces, but as the three become intimates, she moves into the center of their lives, seducing both men with her dreams of escape ("Oh, I'd like to live in a place where the land extends and I can walk for miles, where I can run and never reach the end. Here, there's always the sea. The jail of water."). Pepe, a kindred spirit who deplores Cuba's retrogressive ways (a scarcity of fuel has turned the island into a nation of bicyclists, he whines), hardly needs convincing. Julio, on the other hand, is less eager to be uprooted, but he too falls under

Ines's spell, and as the act ends, he and she are poised not only to take to the seas, but to become lovers as well.

The shift from "Tierra" to "Agua" begets a corresponding shift in style. While the first act is rooted in realism and domestic detail, the second act dispenses with verisimilitude in the interest of a more urgent—if more simply evoked—verism. A bare platform is a stand-in for the raft that bears the trio toward their fate, and with little more accompaniment than Nilo's evocative language, "Agua" depicts a harrowing six-day journey that begins in the external world but slips noiselessly into a hallucinatory one. Nilo is less interested, here as always, in documenting the grim realities of dreams deferred than he is in capturing the soul's buoyant counter-measures, which function not just as compensation for disappointments or dead ends, but as acts of creation in their own right, fulfilling a basic human impulse to recast consciousness itself, even—or perhaps especially—in trauma. Death comes dressed as deliverance in the arms of the sea.

Nilo departs from his usual Cuban milieu in *Lorca in a Green Dress*, an arresting fantasia on the life and legacy of the eponymous Spanish poet and playwright, but he's still very much at home in the setting he has fashioned for his inquiry. For *Lorca in a Green Dress* imagines Lorca in purgatory, not quite released from his earthly existence and not quite ready for spiritual advancement: Lorca, in other words, in one of Nilo's infernal waiting rooms, holding still long enough for Nilo to make a poem of him.

This particular anteroom, a sort of Lorca-themed cabaret by way of Salvador Dalí, is not entirely removed from earth's temporal grip, however. While it offers up shards of the artist's life in a free-wheeling and kaleidoscopic show-and-tell performed for the new arrival by stand-ins assigned to represent various aspects of his being (Lorca in Bicycle Pants, Lorca as a

Woman, Lorca in a White Suit, Lorca in a Green Dress), its point of reference—the wormhole through which everything else in the play must pass—is Lorca's death in 1936 at the hands of the Fascists. Again and again the play returns to that obscenity—the one that has ushered the final Lorca, Lorca with Blood, into the afterlife—until at last the murdered man finds a measure of release within its dark heart.

Lorca in a Green Dress is perhaps the most personal play in this collection, an homage to and collaboration with an artist whose singular voice, equally attuned to the inconsequential pleasures of whimsy and the fathomless weight of woe, puts most of the rest of the modern theatre to shame. The play, with its intensely insider perspective, may be caviar to the general, but el duende, the elusive creative force that Lorca wrote about, lives within its fanciful contours, tasking Nilo at every turn. Near the end of the play, Lorca recalls a happy time spent at the seashore with Dalí and Dalí's sister, Ana María, whom Lorca adored. When Lorca asks them what they do when he's not around, their response is a playful litany: "I say to Dalí, 'Buenos dias without Federico.'" "The maid yells, 'I'm serving breakfast without Federico.'" "Papá says, 'Can you pass me the butter without Federico?'" "And I think to myself, Another day by the sea without Federico." Without Federico. That's the lament behind the play, the sorrow that tinges its music and magic. If Lorca is Spain's open wound, he is Nilo's, too.

Capricho makes a lovely coda to this anthology. A miniature valentine to the theatre, it was one of several site-specific short plays commissioned by the McCarter to celebrate the opening of a second stage, the Berlind Theatre, in 2003. Each of the participating writers (Eric Bogosian, Steven Dietz, Noah Haidle, Joyce Carol Oates, Dael Orlandersmith and Polly Pen, among them) was asked to create a piece for a space of his or her choosing within the theatre complex—options included dressing rooms, rehearsal halls, the wings, the lighting booth, and so

on. (Edward Albee contributed a monologue—more of a S.O.S.,
really—for a theatre critic locked in a closet and unable to get
out. *New York Times* critic Bruce Weber gamely recorded the
Albee speech, which was played in a continuous loop from
behind a closed door in a backstage hallway.) Audiences attend-
ing a community open house were able to tour the facility and
enjoy a serial performance at the same time.

Tucked into a space well off the beaten track, *Capricho* was,
in fact, the only piece not performed in the new building, but in
the trap room of the adjacent old theatre, a cluttered and somewhat shopworn grotto directly below the stage; perfect for a play
about a forgotten understudy waiting in vain for his call. Still
clad in his costume for some long-ago Lope de Vega play and
sweetly oblivious to his companion's skeletal state, he's got a
perpetual case of pre-show jitters. Foolish and forlorn, he's a
leftover trouper, an old world soul doing a ten-minute vaudeville
turn on the virtues of standing by. "Because when we wait," he
explains to the elegantly attired bag of bones at his side, "we see
things we wouldn't see if we weren't waiting, like the slow season of the dust, and this can only be good for the theatre." The
readiness, as Nilo repeatedly reminds us, is all.

*Janice Paran is a New Jersey–based writer and dramaturg. She served
as the McCarter Theatre Center's Director of Play Development from
1991 to 2005.*

TWO
SISTERS
AND
A PIANO

Two Sisters and a Piano premiered on February 16, 1999, at the McCarter Theatre Center (Emily Mann, Artistic Director; Jeffrey Woodward, Managing Director) in Princeton, New Jersey. It was directed by Brian Kulick; the set design was by Mark Wendland, the costume design was by Anita Yavich, the lighting design was by Mimi Jordan Sherin, the sound design was by JR Conklin; the composer was Mark Bennett, the dramaturg was Janice Paran and the production stage manager was Cheryl Mintz. The cast was as follows:

MARÍA CELIA	Ivonne Coll
SOFIA	Marissa Chibas
LIEUTENANT PORTUONDO	Bobby Cannavale
MILITIA GUARD/VICTOR MANUEL	Gary Perez

Two Sisters and a Piano received its West Coast premiere on April 27, 1999, at South Coast Repertory (David Emmes, Producing Artistic Director; Martin Benson, Artistic Director; Paula Tomei, Managing Director) in Costa Mesa, California. It was directed by Loretta Greco; the set design was by Robert Brill, the costume design was by Alex Jaeger, the lighting design was by Geoff Korf, the sound design was by Rob Miller; the stage manager was Randall K. Lum. The cast was as follows:

MARÍA CELIA	Adriana Sevan
SOFIA	Jill Remez
LIEUTENANT PORTUONDO	Carlos Sanz
MILITIA GUARD/VICTOR MANUEL	Javi Mulero

Two Sisters and a Piano was subsequently produced on February 15, 2000, by The Public Theater (George C. Wolfe, Producer; Rosemarie Tichler, Artistic Producer; Michael Litvin, Managing Director) in New York City. It was directed by Loretta Greco; the set design was by Robert Brill, the costume design was by Alex Jaeger, the lighting design was by James Vermeulen, the sound design was by Fabian Obispo; the dramaturg was Shirley Fishman and the production stage manager was Buzz Cohen. The cast was as follows:

MARÍA CELIA	Adriana Sevan
SOPHIA	Daphne Rubin-Vega
LIEUTENANT PORTUONDO/MILITIA GUARD #2	Paul Calderon
MILITIA GUARD #1/VICTOR MANUEL	Gary Perez

CHARACTERS

MARÍA CELIA, the older sister, thirty-six

SOFIA, the younger sister, twenty-four

LIEUTENANT PORTUONDO, a man in his thirties

MILITIA GUARD, thirties

VICTOR MANUEL, a piano tuner, thirties

TIME AND PLACE

Cuba. 1991. A spacious colonial house.

Note to designers: The set and lights should have a feeling of openness. They should not feel claustrophobic.

PROLOGUE

The Search

Music plays. Then, in full darkness, we hear the loud sound of a metal prison door closing. Shadowy lights slowly come up to reveal two militia men in green uniforms at the Obispo house doing a search. The electricity has been cut off. The men hold flashlights, which they aim at different parts of the room. A Victorian sofa and side table are stage left. A baby grand piano is downstage right. The sound of furniture turning over, glass breaking, objects falling on the floor. One of the men, the Militia Guard, pushes Sofia and goes after María Celia.

MILITIA GUARD: Tell us whereyou hide them. Tell us where you keep them.

LIEUTENANT PORTUONDO: Come on, tell us. Come on . . .

MARÍA CELIA: I don't know what you're talking about!

SOFIA: She's not hiding anything!

MILITIA GUARD: Liar . . . You're lying. We want all the papers you're hiding.

SOFIA: She's not hiding any papers.

LIEUTENANT PORTUONDO: Just tell us where you keep them, bitch! Go get your writing.

SOFIA: Don't hurt her or I'll hit you with this chair.

LIEUTENANT PORTUONDO: Just tell us where you hide them.

MARÍA CELIA: Hide what! Hide what!

SOFIA: She's got nothing! She's got nothing! She's not hiding anything!

MARÍA CELIA: I don't have anything.

MILITIA GUARD: You shut up, bitch!

MARÍA CELIA: I already told you . . .

SOFIA: She already told you . . .

MILITIA GUARD: You shut up, you big mouth, or I'll cut off your tongue! I'll cut off your tongue! —Where do you keep your writing?

MARÍA CELIA: I've got nothing! . . . I've got nothing hidden, compañero!

LIEUTENANT PORTUONDO: Let's start the inventory, Mena.

MILITIA GUARD: Who does inspection here every week?

MARÍA CELIA: Polita . . . Polita Mirabal.

MILITIA GUARD (To Lieutenant Portuondo): Polita Mirabal . . . Polita Mirabal.

LIEUTENANT PORTUONDO: The girls have had enough.

MILITIA GUARD: Yeah they've had enough. A bunch of weaklings. We got two lesbos in here. A writer and a pianist. Which one is the pianist? (Sofia raises her hand) Play something on the piano. I have a headache. (Gives Lieutenant Portuondo a file) See if you can figure out these papers. It's a bunch of rice and mangoes. (Walks around, inspecting the rest of the

house with his flashlight) This is a big house for just two
people. Who else you've got living here—ghosts?

LIEUTENANT PORTUONDO: I can't figure out this shit either.

MILITIA GUARD: We'll leave it blank. What's the pianist doing?
I told you to play something.

(Sofia goes to the piano.)

Let's start the inventory. A piano.

LIEUTENANT PORTUONDO: Piano. Check.

MILITIA GUARD: A sofa.

LIEUTENANT PORTUONDO: Sofa. Check.

MILITIA GUARD: A small oak table.

LIEUTENANT PORTUONDO: Oak table. Check.

MILITIA GUARD: A radio.

LIEUTENANT PORTUONDO: Radio. Check.

(Sofia plays the piano.)

MILITIA GUARD: Brass lamp.

LIEUTENANT PORTUONDO: Brass lamp. Check.

(Lights slowly come up on María Celia standing on the rooftop.)

MILITIA GUARD: Rocking chair.

LIEUTENANT PORTUONDO: Rocking chair. Check.

MILITIA GUARD: Record player.

LIEUTENANT PORTUONDO: Record player. Check.

MILITIA GUARD: Picture of a lady with a fan.

LIEUTENANT PORTUONDO: Picture. Check.

*(Lights start to fade on the men. María Celia is in full light
now, holding a letter, which she folds and places in her pocket
as she speaks to her husband in the distance:)*

MARÍA CELIA: "Antonio, my dear husband, I'm standing on top of this roof, wanting to leap into the sky and send you this letter. Almost three months and two weeks now and not a word from you. Today a few militia guards came to search the house. They took inventory of all our things. I don't know what this means. This is usually done when somebody is leaving the country. Yesterday we heard on the radio about amnesty for political prisoners, so I'm keeping my fingers crossed. I tell Sofie that 1991 is our lucky year. We've been allowed back home. At least here we can walk all the way from the kitchen to the living room, and that's a long distance compared to the size of our cell back in prison. It seems that there are so many things happening out there in the world, my love . . . A new way of thinking . . . Freedom . . . I always tell Sofie how much I love the leader Gorbachev (any man who has a birthmark that looks like an island on his forehead is a blessed man). I'm writing a new story, my love, which I'm sending you a page at a time. It's what keeps me going. The writing. The man and the woman in my new story, they take me out of this house. Their walks to the sea. I miss you more and more, my love. A big kiss and a hug, María Celia."

(*Allegro piano music is heard. Lights slowly come up on Sofia playing the piano, as lights fade down on María Celia as she climbs down the spiral staircase from the roof.*)

ACT ONE

Scene 1

THE MAN BEHIND THE WALL AND THE LOST LETTERS

Sofia is playing the piano. María Celia walks toward her. Suddenly, Sofia stops playing.

MARÍA CELIA: Why did you stop?
SOFIA: Shshhh . . .
MARÍA CELIA: But you were playing so beautifully . . .
SOFIA *(Whispering)*: I thought I heard something.
MARÍA CELIA: What?
SOFIA *(Whispering)*: Next door.

(They both speak in low voices:)

MARÍA CELIA: I didn't hear anything. You think he's home? That's probably your imagination. Play that song again.

(Sofia presses her ear to the wall.)

SOFIA *(Whispering)*: No . . . Listen. Come close to the wall.

(María Celia moves close to the wall.)

MARÍA CELIA: I don't hear a thing.
SOFIA: Shshhhh . . . I did. You hear that?

(María Celia walks away from the wall.)

MARÍA CELIA: Nonsense. That's the wind or a cat walking on top
of the roof. There's nobody there.
SOFIA: Yesterday he came around this time. I heard him.
MARÍA CELIA: Where was I?
SOFIA: Where else? You were up on the roof writing.
He sat by the doorway with a drink in his hand. He
smoked and drank and listened to me for more than an hour.
Music is like medicine. I touched his soul.
MARÍA CELIA: Bah. You're falling in love with an invisible man.
SOFIA: You can still love a person and not be physical.
MARÍA CELIA: Then it turns into a lie. A lie of the heart. That's
for young girls who fall in love with a man in a book or a
movie. You're twenty-four years old, and you know very
well that people like him don't like people like us.
SOFIA: You like to press your ear to the wall as much as I do.
MARÍA CELIA: I listen when I'm bored and tired and fed up with
this house. Don't roll your eyes at me. You stand next to
this wall every five minutes. I don't know what could be so
interesting about him.
SOFIA: I heard him tell his friend how much he wanted to lie in
bed with the two of us.
MARÍA CELIA: Yep . . . A rotten, putrid mind he has!
SOFIA: He must see something in us, María Celia.

MARÍA CELIA: Yes I can see what he sees. Two women unable to go out the door, under house arrest. A harem next to his house. —Wake up, Sofia! Can't you see he's a dog! You've heard what he does when he's on duty. He sneaks a woman into the marina. He makes love to her all over his paperwork. Can't you see what kind of man he is—what goes through his head?

SOFIA: I still think it would be an adventure. You on this side of the bed, and me on this other side. We'll drive him wild and crazy, to the point that he'll go to work hypnotized in a trance. Then he'll drop dead from all the rapture, and there on his tomb will be inscribed: HERE I REST IN PEACE FOR LOVING THE OBISPO SISTERS.

MARÍA CELIA: I'm starting to think you have canaries inside your head. Let's go back to work. You're too naive sometimes. The other night I had a dream with Mami. I swear she looked as if she had come down from the sky. I saw her standing at the end of a road, and I could hear her voice, "Celita, my child . . . Sofie, my hummingbird . . . don't let the dirty communists brainwash you . . . don't forget to place a glass of water on the altar for the angels. They get thirsty from watching over you. Teach your sister to walk through life. Pin a prayer to the hem of her dress."

SOFIA: Did she say that? (*Smiles*) Poor Mami . . .

MARÍA CELIA (*Produces a small piece of paper from inside the piano*): I wrote something on a piece of paper. I was going to pin it to your dress without telling you, but then I thought of putting it inside the piano.

SOFIA: What is it?

MARÍA CELIA: A prayer. Let me have the hem of your dress. (*Kneels down to pin it to Sofia's dress*)

(*There is a knock at the door. María Celia goes to the entrance-way and listens. Sofia stays at a distance.*)

SOFIA *(Whispering)*: Who is it?

MARÍA CELIA: Shssh . . . I don't know . . . *(Listens for a moment, then loudly)* Who is it?

LIEUTENANT PORTUONDO: Lieutenant Portuondo, open up.

(María Celia throws up her arms, expressing to her sister the burden of the visit, then opens the door. Lieutenant Portuondo comes in.)

MARÍA CELIA: If you're here for inspection, we had inspection two days ago.

LIEUTENANT PORTUONDO *(Enters the space as if he owned it)*: No. I'm not here for inspection. I came to talk to you.

MARÍA CELIA: What can I do for you, Lieutenant?

LIEUTENANT PORTUONDO: It looks as if you're not well disposed towards visitors, compañera.

MARÍA CELIA: What can I do for you?

LIEUTENANT PORTUONDO *(Takes out an envelope from his knapsack)*: This letter . . .

MARÍA CELIA: I wrote it.

LIEUTENANT PORTUONDO: Well I received it a few days ago . . .

MARÍA CELIA: I sent it to the ministry.

LIEUTENANT PORTUONDO: Then we need to talk. We need to have a private conversation. *(Looks at Sofia. She exits. He strolls around the room)* Your letter is more like a petition or an application. What sort of thing are you applying for?

MARÍA CELIA: I'm asking you to put an end to the postal theft. You hold up all my letters from abroad. You open up all my correspondence, I haven't received a letter from my husband in over three months.

LIEUTENANT PORTUONDO *(Smiles)*: You're absolutely beautiful, compañera. I remember the first day they brought you to the ministry. I couldn't look at you too much. *(Opens file)* I must say this picture on your file doesn't do you justice.

I should try to get a photographer in here and photograph you again.

MARÍA CELIA: I don't like to have my picture taken, Lieutenant. —Can you do something about my mail, or not?

LIEUTENANT PORTUONDO: I suppose I can do a lot about your mail. *(Opens his knapsack and pulls out two packs of letters tied up with a black ribbon)* You receive a considerable amount of correspondence. Dangerous correspondence. Someone found a weapon inside a letter the other day. I was informed that one of our officers at the post office almost bled to death. They found these razor blades inside an envelope. *(Produces razor blades)*

MARÍA CELIA: They shouldn't have gone through my mail.

LIEUTENANT PORTUONDO: Is that a provocation, compañera?

MARÍA CELIA: I just want . . .

LIEUTENANT PORTUONDO: Is somebody sending you razor blades so you can slice someone's throat? Or are you going to do some harm to yourself?

MARÍA CELIA: Those are for my legs, Lieutenant. To shave my legs.

LIEUTENANT PORTUONDO: Our Soviet razors don't cut it for you.

MARÍA CELIA: I thought we were going to talk about my mail.

LIEUTENANT PORTUONDO: We are talking about your mail. The razors—

(Sofia enters.)

SOFIA *(Interrupting)*: Would you like some water, Lieutenant?

LIEUTENANT PORTUONDO: No, thank you, compañera.

SOFIA: María Celia?

MARÍA CELIA: No, thank you.

(Sofia exits.)

LIEUTENANT PORTUONDO: This sort of thing is considered a weapon, illegal . . . Don't you know that?

MARÍA CELIA: I didn't send it, Lieutenant.

LIEUTENANT PORTUONDO *(Pulls out a small sample package of moisturizing lotion)*: I gather this is for your legs too . . . Lotion de rose . . . Smells of roses, France. Who is this Monsieur Lamont? He writes to you often, sends you lots of things. Did you give your legs to this man?

MARÍA CELIA: Look you don't have the right—

LIEUTENANT PORTUONDO: Are you in love with this man?

MARÍA CELIA: I don't think that's important—

LIEUTENANT PORTUONDO: Was he your lover?

MARÍA CELIA: No.

LIEUTENANT PORTUONDO: No?

MARÍA CELIA: He's a friend.

LIEUTENANT PORTUONDO: And all the romantic letters.

MARÍA CELIA: I don't know about any romantic letters.

LIEUTENANT PORTUONDO: You don't know about any romantic letters?

MARÍA CELIA: No, I don't know. How would I know when I don't get any mail?

LIEUTENANT PORTUONDO: You're pretty good at keeping a straight face when you lie. Your husband in America is slipping correspondence through France, using the name André Lamont. I have them all here.

MARÍA CELIA: I don't know what you're talking about.

LIEUTENANT PORTUONDO: You know exactly what I am talking about!

MARÍA CELIA *(With contained anger)*: Why do you keep on insisting that I know, that I know! What am I supposed to know! What am I supposed to do when I live in this hole! *(Pause, then takes hold of herself)* Please—I am not asking for much.

LIEUTENANT PORTUONDO: I can't give you any mail—not when your husband is going to every human rights commission, spreading bile against our system. Not when he's trying to publish your book in France. You must know all about it.

I have all the information here: "Les Editions de Minuit will publish in October the translation of *The Seagrape*, by María Celia Obispo." *(Mockingly)* Imagine, compañera . . . Foi, foi . . . La vie shoo, shoo . . . Just a few months from now your book will be all over France, Europe. Isn't that something, compañera?

Makes me hungry, that name: Minuit. Reminds me of mignon, filet mignon. It's amazing that a word like that can make your mouth water. Means midnight in French, doesn't it? A lot of money, this Minuit company—your father and your husband are going to get rich from your books. Lots of lonely people out there in the world—empty beds . . . I've been reading one of your books. That's my new bed companion. Can you believe it, compañera?

MARÍA CELIA: People should read whatever they like.

LIEUTENANT PORTUONDO: What makes you think I like your books?

MARÍA CELIA: Who cares what I think, Lieutenant? You could be one of those people who reads books to fall asleep at night.

LIEUTENANT PORTUONDO: Oh, I read for meaning, compañera . . . What was that line I like so much in your story? "There was that fugitive night in her." —Is that the way it goes? You don't know what those words do to me.

Does that surprise you, compañera, that I'm reading your book?

MARÍA CELIA: Nothing surprises me, Lieutenant.

LIEUTENANT PORTUONDO: Well, I don't see the big fuss about your books. All the delegations say they're bourgeois propaganda, antirevolutionary. People's blood boils with indignation. But I'm not of the same opinion, I'm probably your number-one fan.

MARÍA CELIA: Oh, just give it up, Lieutenant! I've gone through all the mind games!

(Sofia comes in with a coffee tray.)

SOFIA: Café. I made some café . . . Thought you would like some, Lieutenant.

LIEUTENANT PORTUONDO: Why don't you tell your sister that I didn't come here to do her harm.

SOFIA: I hope not. *(He takes a cup)* If you kill her, she'll come back from the dead. Right, María Celia? *(Smiles, takes sides with her sister)* She'll pull you away by the feet when you're asleep and haunt you for the rest of your life. You don't know my sister.

LIEUTENANT PORTUONDO: Yes, you're right, I don't know your sister. *(Sipping coffee, looking at María Celia)* But I'd sure like to get to know her.

SOFIA: María Celia . . . The lieutenant is talking about you. He wants to get to know you. You want café?

MARÍA CELIA: No.

SOFIA: Is that the mail you have in your knapsack? If you give her the mail you'll be on her good side.

LIEUTENANT PORTUONDO: And what's her good side like?

SOFIA: He wants to know about your good side, María Celia.

MARÍA CELIA: Did you start cooking the beans?

SOFIA: They're cooking. They're cooking all right. *(Looks at Lieutenant Portuondo, then at her sister)* There's a good side to her cooking, I can tell you that much.

LIEUTENANT PORTUONDO: So she's a good cook.

SOFIA: The best chicken fricassee in town.

LIEUTENANT PORTUONDO: Best chicken fricassee.

SOFIA: Get her a chicken. Give her the mail, and she'll make you chicken fricassee.

LIEUTENANT PORTUONDO: Is it true that you're a good cook?

MARÍA CELIA: Am I going to get anything out of this?! Am I going to get my mail or do I have to put myself through a hunger strike?! Do I have to starve to get somebody's attention?!

LIEUTENANT PORTUONDO: I'm sorry, compañera. I can't let you read about your husband's tactics.

MARÍA CELIA: I don't care about his tactics. I just want to know about him. If he's dead or alive, if he's sick or in good health! If he's still my husband for God's sake!

LIEUTENANT PORTUONDO: If he's still your husband! . . . So he is your husband!

MARÍA CELIA: Please . . . compañero, if you don't mind, I'd like you to go now.

LIEUTENANT PORTUONDO: No, I'm not leaving till we finish this talk. Let me give you some advice, compañera . . . You should write a letter to your husband and let him know that all those public denunciations he made, maybe got you out of prison, but that's not going to get you out of this country . . . Do you understand? *(To Sofia)* This concerns you too, Sofia.

(Back to María Celia) If you want to write him about this, I'll make sure your letter gets to him.

MARÍA CELIA: Thank you, Lieutenant.

LIEUTENANT PORTUONDO *(Strolling around the room)*: When do you usually write your stories, compañera?

(Silence. Sofia looks at María Celia, then makes her way over to her.)

SOFIA: She doesn't write, Lieutenant. She stopped writing.

LIEUTENANT PORTUONDO: Oh, I know she writes. Her husband talks about a story she was going to send him. A new story. Something about a man and a woman in a glass tower, stolen boats . . . I want to know if I can read it.

MARÍA CELIA: I never finished it. I threw it away.

LIEUTENANT PORTUONDO: Is it a love story? *(No response)* I'm asking you if it's a love story!

SOFIA: Her stories are always about love, Lieutenant.

LIEUTENANT PORTUONDO *(To Sofia)*: Can I have a moment alone with your sister?

SOFIA: Sure.

(Sofia exits.)

LIEUTENANT PORTUONDO: So what happened to this story?

MARÍA CELIA: I threw it away.

LIEUTENANT PORTUONDO: What if I pay you to write it again?

MARÍA CELIA: That would be a risk, don't you think? Or have you forgotten why we're still locked up in here?

LIEUTENANT PORTUONDO: It seems like everything is—my asking you to accept payment—my standing here talking to you about this . . .

MARÍA CELIA: It's not the same. You are the lieutenant.

LIEUTENANT PORTUONDO: So how can it be done? I want to know about this story. Would you consent to tell me all about it, if I let you have all of these?

(He holds out all the letters.)

MARÍA CELIA: That would certainly compromise you, if you let me have all the letters.

LIEUTENANT PORTUONDO: You're right. But I can always read them to you.

MARÍA CELIA: Then you don't want any evidence either. It has to be a clean crime.

LIEUTENANT PORTUONDO: Well, if you want to put it that way— I'm willing to read you the letters.

MARÍA CELIA: I have more to lose than you do. You know that.

LIEUTENANT PORTUONDO: Why don't you think about it. You don't have to give me an answer now.

Good day, compañera!

(He exits.)

MARÍA CELIA (*In a loud voice*): Sofia, are you there?

(*Sofia comes out.*)

Were you listening? Did you see all those letters? Did you see the whole pack? Hundreds of them.

SOFIA: I knew Antonio hadn't forgotten you. I knew.

(*The lights fade to black.*)

Scene 2

THE BEDSPREADS OF DESIRE

Daytime. Soft, grayish white lights. It is raining outside. María Celia is reciting a letter to her husband:

MARÍA CELIA: "My dear love, It's no longer a secret, the Ministry is holding up your letters. Every part of me, even my fury and rancor, is being registered and kept in a file. Now they're keeping your letters to document the weight of my heart. Today when I woke up and washed my face . . ." (*Touches her face*) "I thought that perhaps when you see me again, I'll be less than you expected, that you'll find me less beautiful. I'm thirty-six years old and I feel my life is evaporating in front of me, that I'm rotting and decaying in this house . . . It's the thought of you, the strength of your eyes that brings the precipitation of life . . . I kiss you all over, María Celia . . ."

(*Lights up on Sofia and María Celia knitting.*)

SOFIA: We're almost out of the good yarn.

MARÍA CELIA: What's wrong with this other yarn?

SOFIA: It's tough on my hands. It's like steel wool for scouring pots. You start weaving and purling with that thing and you'll end up with minced meat for hands.

MARÍA CELIA: That's the only yarn we have left.

SOFIA: I have to protect my hands.

MARÍA CELIA: Use a pair of gloves. If we don't knit there won't be any bedspreads. And if there's no bedspreads, what are we going to give Cirilo to sell?

SOFIA: It's days like this I could play the piano the whole day.

MARÍA CELIA: I bet. You tell me that every day.

SOFIA: I can't play it anymore. The piano is falling apart.

MARÍA CELIA: What about the permit you got to have it tuned?

SOFIA: I sent for a piano tuner—hasn't shown up.

MARÍA CELIA: Give it some time.

SOFIA: Look at my hands, veins starting to show up from all this knitting. That's always been my fear. On men the veins look good. On men yes—because it makes them look strong and virile, like their plumbing works well and lots of blood flows through all their parts. I hate these needles. I hate all this knitting.

MARÍA CELIA: I know. You tell me every time we knit.

SOFIA: Oscarito had lots of veins like a Roman aqueduct. Everywhere. I loved how they showed his strength. All the rivers from his heart. Oh, I wish I had a glass of rum with ice. A man . . . A man, is what I wish I had . . . I loved doing it when it rained. *(Stretches)*

MARÍA CELIA: You sound like a cat in heat.

SOFIA: Take a break for God's sake! I don't know where you get all that energy, when all we had to eat were eggs and mangoes.

MARÍA CELIA: I'm tired but I keep at it. I keep at it.

SOFIA: If that lieutenant comes again you should ask him if he could get us something to eat.

MARÍA CELIA: I told you I'm not going to ask him for food.

SOFIA: Why not? He could make life easier for us.

MARÍA CELIA: No. I've been thinking of having him read me the letters and that's all. I'm not going to give him any papers. I'm just going to tell him the story.

SOFIA: I wouldn't do it. He'll find something in it. It always happens.

MARÍA CELIA: What could he possibly find? It's a simple love story for God's sake!

SOFIA: He could testify against you. You keep me out of it.

MARÍA CELIA: Keep you out of it?! And you want me to ask him for food!

SOFIA: Well, we have it bad as it is. I don't want anything else to do with your writing.

MARÍA CELIA: I can't believe the things that come out of your mouth! You might as well turn me in.

SOFIA: I can't go back to the prison! Not back there, you hear me . . . I'd rather be in a hole, underground, full of worms. Every night I have nightmares about that place. I wake up out of breath, like a lost animal . . .

MARÍA CELIA: Forget I said anything. Do you remember when you were playing that song on the piano?

SOFIA: Which one?

MARÍA CELIA: "La Savane." *(The music of Gottschalk is heard)* I'd never heard it that way before. The whole music . . . I felt as if I had to leave my body. I went to the sea. Next minute, I was writing about this man and this woman in the marina. The story had gotten inside me like a sickness. For three days I stayed up at night writing.

SOFIA: Are you the woman in this story?

MARÍA CELIA: No.

SOFIA: And him?

MARÍA CELIA: He's like the man next door.

SOFIA: The man next door? Why him?

MARÍA CELIA: I don't know. It all came to me that day. —The woman in the story goes to visit him at the marina when

21

he's on duty. She always tells him that she wants to know about the sea . . . She wants to learn from him. The first night she goes to him, she asks if he eats alone, and he tells her that he does. She tells him it's sad to see men having dinner alone. A person should never eat alone. She asks him if she could cook for him. That they could have dinner together overlooking the sea.

SOFIA: Does he accept?

MARÍA CELIA: He's not allowed to receive visitors when he's on duty. But she tells him that she wouldn't be a visitor, she'd only come to bring him food.

SOFIA: That'd be something I would say. And I would show up to see him even if he said no. I'd show up in a white dress.

MARÍA CELIA: She wears a white dress.

SOFIA: Maybe a long blue scarf, to go with the sea, white sandals and a parasol.

MARÍA CELIA: It's nighttime, Sofie. Why would she have a parasol?

SOFIA: That's true. You said it was nighttime. I'm sorry. You took me there with the story. (Laughs) —Do you realize this is going to be another summer that we won't be able to go to the sea?

MARÍA CELIA: Yes. I know.

SOFIA: I was sitting there with him at the marina with a picnic basket. My feet dangling from the pier . . . And me occasionally dipping my toes in the water, then looking at him.

MARÍA CELIA: They meet on a tower, Sofie. A glass tower and it's not a picnic.

SOFIA: Go on. Don't mind me. I'm making your story into something else.

MARÍA CELIA: Now I forgot where I was.

SOFIA: The glass tower.

MARÍA CELIA: Yes, the glass tower surrounded by blue boats . . . Fishermen retrieving their nets from the sea. Seagulls.

SOFIA: Yes, lots of seagulls.

MARÍA CELIA: The woman walks by the sea taking puffs from her cigarette, leaving smoke behind like a steamship. She climbs the stairs to the glass tower. She goes to see him, with her purse full of bread, rice, plantains, beans, boiled eggs, avocados, guava marmalade, napkins, forks, spoons, salt and pepper. A whole restaurant in her little bag.

SOFIA: That should be the name of the story: "Picnic by the Light of the Moon." I guess you can tell him all about it. What could be wrong with a picnic in a marina? But don't show him any writing.

VICTOR MANUEL (*Offstage*): Sofia . . .

(*The sisters look at each other.*)

SOFIA: Someone called my name.

(*There's a knock at the door.*)

VICTOR MANUEL (*Offstage*): Sofia . . .

MARÍA CELIA: Who is it?

VICTOR MANUEL (*Offstage*): Victor Manuel.

MARÍA CELIA: Who?

VICTOR MANUEL (*Offstage*): Victor Manuel . . . I came to take a look at the piano.

(*There is a pause. The sisters look at each other again.*)

SOFIA: Yes . . . yes . . . Coming . . . coming . . . It's the piano tuner . . . The piano tuner . . . And me looking like a mess! Do I look all right?

MARÍA CELIA: Open the door . . .

VICTOR MANUEL (*Offstage*): Open up . . . It's raining up a storm out here.

(Sofia rushes to the door. She fixes her hair a little and looks down at her clothes to see if she's presentable. She opens the door. Victor Manuel enters, carrying his tool bag.)

What a storm ... what a storm ... It's a monsoon out there.

(He notices Sofia. He reaches out for her hand.)

Polita sent me here with this permit. She told me the piano needs tuning. *(Takes out a handkerchief)* Which one is Sofia?

SOFIA: Me. I'm Sofia.

VICTOR MANUEL: I'm Victor Manuel.

MARÍA CELIA: And I'm María Celia, her sister.

VICTOR MANUEL *(Shaking her hand)*: At your service, compañera.

(Sofia stares at him. She becomes nervous. An awkward pause.)

SOFIA: The piano is right here. We didn't know you were coming. *(Uncovers the piano)* My sister covered it as if it was a child. *(He looks at her)* Humidity!

(He plays the piano, then plays individual keys.)

VICTOR MANUEL: Yes, it sounds bad. *(Key)* Yes, bad. *(Key)* Bad. *(Key)* Bad. *(Key)* It buzzes a little. Hear that ... *(Key)* I'll have to check the soundboard and the ribs. *(Takes out a flashlight from his pocket and inspects underneath the piano)* When was the last time you had the piano tuned?

SOFIA: I guess more than two years ago. *(Looks at her sister)*

VICTOR MANUEL: Neglect ruins a piano, compañera. It's in real bad shape. When a piano is neglected it dies. It's like a plant, a tree. When you don't water a tree it withers away. *(Takes tools out of his bag, continues inspecting the inside of the piano)* I always say there should be mandatory rules for the use of pianos. If they are not being played . . . if they're not being put to good use, they should be donated to schools, hospitals, recreational parks. The Interior Ministry should intervene in this matter. Take inventory of all the pianos in the city, number them all and place them into categories: "the so-and-so family, living at such-and-such address makes use of their piano"; "the so-and-so family, at this other address uses the piano for family pictures and ashtrays." That's the only way we're going to get rid of the old system of using pianos for decoration. The old way of showing wealth and social class, through a piano in the living room.

MARÍA CELIA: We're not bourgeois, compañero, if that's what you're implying.

VICTOR MANUEL: I'm talking to myself, compañera. I'm talking to myself.

(To Sofia now) There's some rust and corrosion on the metal parts. Some of the felt has to be changed . . . some of the wires have to be replaced. You also have to change some of the wood in the bottom . . . See in there . . .

SOFIA: What's wrong with it?

VICTOR MANUEL: It's rotting. It looks like water got inside the piano.

MARÍA CELIA: The dogs got in here, wrecked the whole place, stole things when the house got closed up. It's a good thing they didn't take an ax and chop it to pieces.

SOFIA: María Celia . . . please . . . (To Victor Manuel) So what should we do? Can you fix it?

VICTOR MANUEL: Well I suppose I can fix some things. As far as the wood in the bottom, that would mean dismantling some parts and having them custom-made. That will mean sending the piano to a repair place, where they can do that kind of work.

SOFIA: Where is this place?

VICTOR MANUEL: The only one I know is in the Orient.

SOFIA: Well, if it needs to be sent there . . .

MARÍA CELIA: That's like saying the Himalayas. It would cost a fortune. We don't have that kind of money. —Can't you fix it somehow and make it sound pretty again?

VICTOR MANUEL: Well, I can certainly try. I'm just telling you about the major problems.

MARÍA CELIA: You haven't told us how much you'll charge us.

VICTOR MANUEL: Twenty . . .

MARÍA CELIA: Twenty? That's a lot of money.

VICTOR MANUEL: That's how much I charge.

MARÍA CELIA: Ten pesos. That's how much we can afford.

VICTOR MANUEL: Compañera, that's not enough to buy a can of sardines. How about five dollars? —Five if you have dollars.

MARÍA CELIA: We don't have dollars, and that's too much money for just pulling a couple of strings.

VICTOR MANUEL (*Starts placing his tools in his bag*): Well, that takes care of that. Perhaps I should leave. You're wasting my time . . . And time is money. Money you won't spare. Money you don't have.

SOFIA: No . . . Please. Don't leave. Wait one second.

(Sofia exits. Victor Manuel looks at María Celia.)

VICTOR MANUEL: Where is she going? What is she going to do? I can't be wasting my time. I have other appointments. With all the celebrations for the Pan-American games, everybody wants their pianos tuned. You know it's the big event this year. Parties everywhere. There's people here from all over the world. —I'm sorry. Here I am carrying on and you stuck in this house . . .

MARÍA CELIA: It's all right, compañero. It's all right . . .

VICTOR MANUEL: It's a shame what happened to you and your sister. You know, I've read some of your stories. The one about the woman who walks into the sea. I never thought the books were . . . you know . . .

MARÍA CELIA: What?

VICTOR MANUEL: I mean . . . the books . . . It's a shame you started writing other kinds of material.

MARÍA CELIA: What are you trying to get at, compañero?

VICTOR MANUEL: I mean . . . the . . . the new material . . . your new stories. Your views, compañera. How you changed your opinion about the revolution.

MARÍA CELIA: Is this an interrogation, compañero?

VICTOR MANUEL: No, of course not. Why would you say that?

MARÍA CELIA: Then why all the little questions?

VICTOR MANUEL: I'm . . . compañera, please, I didn't mean to pry. Polita asked me to come and tune the piano . . . she gave me this permit.

MARÍA CELIA: Anybody can say that, compañero. Anybody can grab a doctor's bag like yours . . .

VICTOR MANUEL: Now look! . . . look, I can show you my identity card.

MARÍA CELIA: What identity card? The government can fabricate those in a blink. How do I know you don't have a recording machine inside your doctor's bag, under your shirt?

VICTOR MANUEL (*Opens the tool bag, furiously*): Look . . . I don't . . . I don't . . . (*Shows her the tool bag and drops it on the floor. He opens his shirt and shows her his belly*) Look . . . you can see . . . I have nothing under my shirt. (*María Celia doesn't look*)

(*Sofia enters with a shoebox.*)

You want to look inside my pants? You want to see inside my pants? (*Starts to unfasten his pants*)

SOFIA: What's going on?

VICTOR MANUEL: Your sister wants to look inside my pants! She says I'm an informer. Now here's my identity card. So, have

I wasted my time by coming here or are you going to tune the piano?

SOFIA: Yes, of course. María Celia, please . . .

MARÍA CELIA: We can afford only ten pesos. That's all we can afford.

(María Celia exits. Sofia looks at Victor Manuel. She kneels down and opens the shoebox.)

SOFIA: I wanted to know if these shoes fit you. They're new. They belonged to my father. I thought this would make up for the rest of the money we don't have.

VICTOR MANUEL *(Closes his eyes in disbelief)*: Ave María purisima!

SOFIA: Please . . . these are almost brand-new. If the shoes don't fit, you can always sell them.

(Victor Manuel tries to control himself. He brings his hand to his forehead, trying to make sense of the situation. Sofia tries to take off his shoes.)

Please try them on.

VICTOR MANUEL: What are you doing?

SOFIA: What size do you wear? *(Gently tries to lift up his foot)* I think these are a nine-and-a-half. Is that your size?

VICTOR MANUEL: No thank you, compañera. I wear a nine. Don't touch . . .

SOFIA: They'll fit you. These are nine-and-a-half. *(Trying to take off his shoes)*

VICTOR MANUEL: Please, compañera, don't . . . please, lady, don't . . . please . . . don't touch . . . my feet are ticklish . . . *(Tries to keep from laughing)* Don't . . . *(Laughs)* . . . Don't touch my feet, please . . . *(Tries on the shoes)* I can put them on by myself! . . . I never let anybody touch my feet!

SOFIA: How do they fit?

VICTOR MANUEL: The left one feels . . .

SOFIA: Good leather.

VICTOR MANUEL: Well . . . I . . . I don't . . . *(Feels the comfort of the shoes)* They actually . . . I . . . I mean . . . I can actually use a new pair of shoes. *(Walks around the room to get a feel for the shoes)* You have nothing to worry about . . . We'll give the piano a quick fix. The rest can be solved later. If a 1956 Chevy can run with Soviet parts, I can make this piano sound like a concert grand.

(Victor Manuel goes for his tool bag and opens it. There is a knock at the door. He looks at Sofia. Sofia is motionless.)

LIEUTENANT PORTUONDO *(Offstage)*: Can't you see the puddle, jerk! The streets aren't just for cars. *(Knocks again)* María Celia . . .

(One more knock. Sofia goes to open the door. Lieutenant Portuondo comes in, carrying a package and a paper bag. He speaks rapidly as he takes off his raincoat.)

(Straightening his clothes) —What a storm out there! We'll be swimming like fish by the time September gets here . . . *(Opens the paper bag)* I brought some food, maybe it got all wet.

(Lieutenant Portuondo looks up and notices Victor Manuel. He's surprised to see him. He becomes more formal.)

SOFIA: He's tuning the piano.

LIEUTENANT PORTUONDO: Can I see your identity card, compañero?

SOFIA: He's got a permit. He's got a permit from one of the inspectors to tune the piano.

VICTOR MANUEL *(Showing him the permit)*: Just servicing the piano, compañero. Just here for work.

(María Celia enters the room.)

SOFIA: The lieutenant is here to see you, María Celia.

MARÍA CELIA: Good afternoon, Lieutenant.

LIEUTENANT PORTUONDO: Good afternoon, compañera. Thank you, compañero. *(Gives him back the card)*

MARÍA CELIA: Come this way, Lieutenant.

(Lieutenant Portuondo and María Celia move to the sofa at the other side of the room. The lights shift to them.)

Did you think we hired a piano tuner without a permit from the inspectors?

LIEUTENANT PORTUONDO: Just doing my job, compañera. *(Giving her the bag)* I brought you some food. I know it's hard to get food nowadays.

MARÍA CELIA: That's kind of you, Lieutenant.

LIEUTENANT PORTUONDO: Also brought you these books, thought you might like to read them. *(Gives her the books)* Simone de Beauvoir. Have you read her?

MARÍA CELIA: Not this one.

LIEUTENANT PORTUONDO: Good. Now you have a book to read.

MARÍA CELIA: And this book on Perestroika?

LIEUTENANT PORTUONDO: What about it?

MARÍA CELIA: Why are you giving me this book? Are you testing me, Lieutenant?

LIEUTENANT PORTUONDO: No. Not at all. You're too suspicious, compañera. Don't you like Perestroika? Didn't you and all your artist friends write a manifesto about Perestroika?

MARÍA CELIA: It got me in prison. I have this book.

LIEUTENANT PORTUONDO: Then I'll take it back.

MARÍA CELIA: Wasn't it also taken off the shelves? I had to buy it from someone off the streets—exchanged a whole bag of rice for it.

LIEUTENANT PORTUONDO: That's almost a month of rice on your table.

MARÍA CELIA: It's food for thought, Lieutenant. What we've forgotten in this island—to feed the mind. The fact that there are revolutions within revolutions. Are you recording what I'm saying? Is this why you brought these books, for me to run my mouth, and see if I've gone through political rehabilitation?

LIEUTENANT PORTUONDO: No. Not at all. On the contrary, I'm giving them to you because I thought you would like them. The one with the blue cover, this poet always writes about the sea, like you. I'll pretend I never gave them to you. I'm not a demon, compañera. I hope with time you'll learn to trust me. See, I trust you, already. *(Pulls out a letter from his pocket)* I brought you a letter from your husband. I can read you part of it. Full letter if you decide to go ahead with the agreement. Would you like me to read you some?

MARÍA CELIA: If you like.

(He looks at her. He opens the letter. She closes her eyes. Piano music swells, perhaps "Waltz of the Shadows" by Lecuona. The lights fade on María Celia and Lieutenant Portuondo, then slowly come up on the other side of the room. Victor Manuel is playing the piano. Sofia stands next to him lost in the music. After a while the song finishes.)

SOFIA: What is it about that song? It just goes right to your soul. Why isn't this kind of music played on the radio? Why are we neglecting it?

VICTOR MANUEL: Oh, I don't neglect it. It's my favorite song. I play it all the time.

SOFIA: You do. But try playing it in public and people will say that you're bourgeois and sentimental . . . We don't play Lecuona because he was too romantic, Gershwin because he was

American, Chopin because he was European. It's like
everything old reeks of death. But how can one talk about
these things, Victor Manuel?

VICTOR MANUEL: Well . . . I . . . I . . . I don't know . . . I.

SOFIA: Does it make you uncomfortable to talk about it?

VICTOR MANUEL: No . . . no . . . I play what I like in my house.
I play this kind of music all the time. It's what I love. I don't
know about other people but I still play it.

SOFIA: How come I never met you before?

VICTOR MANUEL: Oh, I don't know, I used to work at Carrion's
piano store, before it burned down.

SOFIA: Yes . . . I remember when it happened, couldn't walk
through the street after the fire. I couldn't bear to see all
those melted pianos.

VICTOR MANUEL: Well, I should be running along. I really ought
to be going. It's raining less now . . .

SOFIA: Please, stay with me a while longer. It's not every day I get
to talk about the music I love. And sometimes, you never
know who you can talk to. But you . . . My sister says I'm a
fool because I trust any person who comes in here and
stands in front of me . . . because I speak my mind . . .
because I haven't lost the habit of saying things the way
they're meant to be said . . . When you came here I thought
. . . I thought . . .

VICTOR MANUEL: That I came to interrogate you . . .

SOFIA: You talked about the inventory of pianos. For a moment
I thought you were going to . . .

VICTOR MANUEL: Take away the piano? No. I wouldn't. I wouldn't
do that to you.

SOFIA (Touches the piano): More than ninety years living in this
house. Part of the family. My mother played it, my grand-
father. He's like an old uncle. Probably the only one who
still takes me out for a walk. Would you come back?
(Holding his hand) Why don't you come back tomorrow?

VICTOR MANUEL: Look, I'd . . . I'd like to . . . but I don't know . . . You and your sister . . . This permit . . .

SOFIA: You can always say you haven't finished tuning the piano. You have a permit.

VICTOR MANUEL: I mean . . . I wouldn't know . . . It's difficult . . . it's risking . . .

SOFIA *(There are tears in her eyes)*: I understand.

VICTOR MANUEL: Look, I would like to. I like talking to you.

(Pause.)

(Gently lifting up her chin) Please, you're making me feel . . .

SOFIA *(More contained)*: It's all right. I understand.

(Silence. He gathers his tools and places them inside his tool bag. He looks at her.)

VICTOR MANUEL: How about next week, I'll be less busy. The end of the games. I'll try to come.

SOFIA: All right.

(She kisses him.)

VICTOR MANUEL: Tuesday then.

(He walks to the doorway. Then he turns to her and waves good-bye. The lights change to María Celia sitting on a chair. Lieutenant Portuondo stands behind her.)

MARÍA CELIA: Would you read me part of another letter, Lieutenant?

LIEUTENANT PORTUONDO: If you want. *(Looks at her. He opens another letter and begins to read)* "My dear love, A few moments ago I woke up, and walked to the store to buy writing paper, and I stopped by the bay. I stood there facing the water thinking of you."

MARÍA CELIA: Please, read slower . . .

(He looks at her. María Celia closes her eyes.)

LIEUTENANT PORTUONDO: "I remembered how much you like to sit by the seawall and write for hours. The whole blue landscape had me holding your arms, your whole body once again. How I love your skin, your smell . . ."

MARÍA CELIA: Slower . . .

LIEUTENANT PORTUONDO: How much slower do you want me to read?

MARÍA CELIA: Just a little slower if you're not going to read me the whole thing. *(Closes her eyes to listen)*

LIEUTENANT PORTUONDO: "I spent a couple of weeks in Sweden. I wonder if you got my postcard. I bought you a beautiful book on butterflies. I know how much you like them. Such a long time since I heard from you last. I've been in absolute torture for months now, but I don't let the dogs eat away at my hopes to see you again. I go nuts counting every day and week that goes by, and I just want the moment to come when I can have you free." *(No longer reading the letter, but looking at her)* I close my eyes and try to imagine that day, when I can undress you like the first time and discover you all over again. Enter every secret place in your body. I want to make love for weeks and months, make up for all the lost time.

MARÍA CELIA: You can stop now. *(He pretends to be reading)* You can stop.

LIEUTENANT PORTUONDO: Are you all right, compañera?

MARÍA CELIA: Yes.

LIEUTENANT PORTUONDO: Would you tell me a little bit of your story?

(Pause. She looks at him.)

MARÍA CELIA: It begins with the sultry months of summer. The man from the marina would call the woman and tell her not to come, that it'd be impossible for her to visit him. He had to be up on his feet keeping an eye out for lost ships. But the woman would disregard the calls, and show up to see him. She had thieves come to the marina and steal boats while she was upstairs in the tower. The rain, the storms made it easier to steal the boats. She'd tell the man about the foghorns, how the sound would make her sad. The wailing of the ships out there in the middle of the sea, and him in the tower alone like those ships . . . she'd get the urge to go . . . —That's all for now.

LIEUTENANT PORTUONDO *(Folds the letter)*: Your husband is mad about you.

MARÍA CELIA: He misses me.

LIEUTENANT PORTUONDO: I don't blame him. I would miss you, too, if I were him. Have a good afternoon, compañera.

(Lieutenant Portuondo exits. The stage is fully lit now. María Celia sits on the sofa. Sofia runs to her.)

SOFIA: María Celia, what did he bring us?

MARÍA CELIA *(Lost in thought)*: He read me part of a letter. I wish you could've heard him read it to me. For a moment I thought Antonio was in the room.

SOFIA: What did he have to say?

MARÍA CELIA: Oh, Sofie, you know the secret codes Antonio uses in his letters, the butterflies . . .

SOFIA: Yes.

MARÍA CELIA: He's been to Sweden.

SOFIA: Sweden?

MARÍA CELIA: Yes. He's trying to find us political asylum there. He said he bought me a book on butterflies and that's what it means. He's still trying to get us out . . .

SOFIA: So when did he say?

MARÍA CELIA: The lieutenant didn't read me the whole thing.

SOFIA: Why not?

MARÍA CELIA: There was probably information they don't want me to know. *(Pause)* If I tell the lieutenant about my new writing, I want you to be in the room when he reads me the letters. I want you to be a witness.

SOFIA: Anything you want.

MARÍA CELIA: Sooner than we think, tear down these walls and walk out of this house. Soon we'll be free.

(The music of Lecuona plays, perhaps "Andalucía." The lights fade to black.)

Act Two

Scene 1

Waiting for Him on Top of My Roof

Evening. We hear music. The lights slowly come up on Sofia sitting on a chair. She wears a simple colorful dress. María Celia stands behind her, combing her hair. Sofia is applying lipstick and looks into a small compact mirror. María Celia's mind wanders to her letter writing while she combs her sister's hair.

MARÍA CELIA: "My dear love, I write to you in my mind, on my skin, even when I go about doing housework. Tonight Sofie has invited to dinner the man who tuned the piano—not that we can afford another dish on our table, but we'll have a visitor for a change."

(Sofia gets up and climbs the spiral staircase to the roof. She stares into the distance waiting for Victor Manuel. María

Celia walks around the room with a cloth, dusting the sofa and the piano.)

"There are fewer and fewer products in the markets these days. We're running out of everything. We use milk of magnesia for deodorant. Soon we'll be out of lipstick and have to use beet juice to color our lips. I probably sound vain, because lipstick isn't necessary, but it's good to add a touch of red to the face for those blue days."

SOFIA *(Shouting)*: María Celia . . . I think I see him coming . . . Warm up the food . . . He's walking down the street . . .

MARÍA CELIA *(In a loud voice)*: Shouldn't I wait till he's actually here? This is the third time I've warmed up the food.

SOFIA: I think it's him walking this way . . .

MARÍA CELIA: Are you sure this time? It's almost 9:30 now.

SOFIA: It's got to be him.

MARÍA CELIA: Just come down, Sofie . . . come down . . .

SOFIA: Wait . . . first I want to see . . .

MARÍA CELIA: You've been up and down from that roof the whole night.

SOFIA: He's crossing the street now . . .

MARÍA CELIA: Is it him?

SOFIA *(Climbs down from the roof)*: You're right, he's not coming . . . It wasn't him.

MARÍA CELIA: Oh, Sofie, maybe something happened. Don't get that way. Maybe he went to one of the games. You know how men are, they are like children when it comes to sports. Maybe he's afraid of being seen here. Come on, cheer up . . . You and I will have dinner. I'm going to play a record, we'll have a good time. I want you to dance with me. Come on . . . *(Goes behind the sofa to their record player and puts on a fast Cuban song)* Dance with me . . . dance . . .

(The music livens up the mood. María Celia starts dancing with Sofia . . . Sofia gives in to the dance, and the sisters start showing off their best steps and turns. They laugh, enjoying their dancing.

There is a knock at the door. María Celia turns off the music. There is another knock. Sofia fixes her hair and clothes and goes to open the door, expecting the piano tuner. Lieutenant Portuondo enters dressed in a summer suit. He's carrying a bottle.)

LIEUTENANT PORTUONDO: Listening to music?

SOFIA: Yes . . . we . . . we were . . .

(Pause.)

LIEUTENANT PORTUONDO: Celebrating the end of the Pan-American Games?

SOFIA AND MARÍA CELIA: No . . .

MARÍA CELIA: We're . . . just . . . just listening to some records . . .

LIEUTENANT PORTUONDO: You're all dressed up this evening.

MARÍA CELIA *(Nervously)*: We are . . . aren't we? . . . Get tired of the same clothes.

LIEUTENANT PORTUONDO: I brought some rum, thought maybe you'd like to have a drink with me.

SOFIA: No. You'll have to excuse me, Lieutenant, I'm going to bed.

MARÍA CELIA: Stay up a while longer.

LIEUTENANT PORTUONDO: Have a drink with us. *(To María Celia)* Would you bring some glasses? It's a night for celebration. We won over seventy medals in the games. We beat the Americans in almost everything. Can you believe it?

SOFIA: Our radio is broken, Lieutenant. We don't get any news. We don't know what's happening out there in the world.

LIEUTENANT PORTUONDO: You should give it to me. I'll have it fixed.

(María Celia gives him the glasses. He opens the bottle.)

MARÍA CELIA: No. You don't have to, Lieutenant.

LIEUTENANT PORTUONDO: I'll fix it for you. I know someone who fixes radios. *(Pours the rum)* Sweet poison, this rum. Everywhere there are tourists drinking tonight, burning their guts out. Can you hear the drums? They make the island come alive. They release things from inside people. *(Raises his glass)* Salud.

MARÍA CELIA: Salud. *(Smells the rum, takes a sip)*

SOFIA: Salud.

MARÍA CELIA: I haven't had rum in so long, forgot what it tastes like.

SOFIA: Me, too.

LIEUTENANT PORTUONDO: Well, drink up. I brought a whole bottle.

SOFIA: It seems like the whole island is out tonight. How come you're not out celebrating?

LIEUTENANT PORTUONDO: Because I wanted to see the two of you.

SOFIA: An odd place to visit. Not even the moon comes to this house.

LIEUTENANT PORTUONDO: Well, that's the moon for you. I like visiting you.

MARÍA CELIA: If it weren't this late I'd go out into the patio and pull a few mint leaves from our plants. A little mint would give the rum the finishing touch.

LIEUTENANT PORTUONDO: What's the matter, you're afraid of the darkness? Tell me where the mint plant is. I'll pull a few leaves.

MARÍA CELIA: No. It's not good to disturb the plants at this hour. It's an old African belief—respect for the night, the plants . . . Our mother used to say:

MARÍA CELIA AND SOFIA *(Laughing)*: "Never ask a tree for fruit at night, because the whole wilderness sleeps after sundown."

LIEUTENANT PORTUONDO: You fascinate me, compañera.

SOFIA: That was our mother, Lieutenant.

LIEUTENANT PORTUONDO: Well I think the two of you are fascinating.

SOFIA: No. Not like she was.

MARÍA CELIA: She was a lovely woman, Lieutenant.

SOFIA: Yes, she was.

MARÍA CELIA: Every time she entered the patio out there, all the plants rejoiced in her presence.

SOFIA: And here in this room, every afternoon she'd sit to play the piano and the whole neighborhood would quiet down to listen to her music.

LIEUTENANT PORTUONDO: So talent runs in the family, you and your mother played the piano and María Celia writes . . . How about your father?

SOFIA: He was an accountant . . .

MARÍA CELIA: Someone had to do the numbers.

SOFIA: Oh, we can tell you stories about our family—

MARÍA CELIA: Every day we discover things about Mamá for the first time—

SOFIA: Why her room was on the east side of the house—

MARÍA CELIA: Because she loved the morning light.

SOFIA: Why she used to write prayers on the soles of our shoes.

MARÍA CELIA: Why she had her own views about the revolution.

LIEUTENANT PORTUONDO: She was a revolutionary?

SOFIA: Maybe not the kind you would like.

MARÍA CELIA: We've always been revolutionary, Lieutenant. The whole family.

LIEUTENANT PORTUONDO: So why did your father leave the country?

SOFIA: He felt he couldn't speak his mind.

LIEUTENANT PORTUONDO: I see. I suppose it can be difficult sometimes.

SOFIA: You suppose right enough.

LIEUTENANT PORTUONDO: My old man . . . he left just like your father.

SOFIA: He did.

LIEUTENANT PORTUONDO: Got fed up one day and said: "This isn't going anywhere." Got tired of waiting. He wanted to take me with him.

SOFIA: You?

LIEUTENANT PORTUONDO: Yes. But I was already in the military.

MARÍA CELIA: I can't imagine you living up North.

LIEUTENANT PORTUONDO: Well sometimes I wonder what my life would've been like if I'd left. The poor man, ended up in some snowy town. Never married again after my mother died. He used to say he was old and didn't have any more heart left in him. —Was a good man, my father. Hard worker . . . Had an old Buick, used to travel the whole island selling milk containers to farmers. I used to help him on the road. Many a time, I saw his eyes water, when an old bolero used to play on the radio, and I'd ask him, "Why you crying, Pipo?" And he'd say, "I just saw Pucha, your mother, through the mirror." And I'd turn around to look and there'd be no one on the backseat. And he'd keep on telling me, "Oh, I know she's there, I can smell her sweet powder." It used to give me the creeps.

MARÍA CELIA: Why?

LIEUTENANT PORTUONDO: Knowing my father, he'd let go of the steering wheel and jump on the backseat with her.

(The sisters laugh.)

More rum?

MARÍA CELIA: Just a bit.

(He pours some rum in María Celia's glass.)

LIEUTENANT PORTUONDO: You know, every time I come to this house I seem to forget the world. Something about you and your sister. You're different.

(He pours some rum in Sofia's glass.)

SOFIA: I'm sure we are, especially now in Mamá's clothes.

LIEUTENANT PORTUONDO: No, what I'm talking about is something in the blood.

MARÍA CELIA: In the blood?

LIEUTENANT PORTUONDO: Yes. What is it? What is that something that is passed on, that makes us who we are? I mean intelligence . . . grace . . . you're pure . . . You are who you are, unlike me. I don't know what I'm saying . . . ey, what would I know! I come from the middle of nowhere. A miserable town made of mud. Houses made of palm leaves. Dirt floor. No running water. I think people die there from looking at the cows. You know the only thing I liked about that place were the hurricanes. I loved the hurricanes. I was always waiting for the wind to blow hard enough and blow me away from there.

(He drinks. Sound of voices coming from the outside, firecrackers.)

MARÍA CELIA: What is that noise?

LIEUTENANT PORTUONDO: It must be the people going home from the stadium.

SOFIA: They sound happy and cheerful.

MARÍA CELIA: They do.

(Pause.)

Did anybody see you come in here at this hour? There's always somebody keeping an eye on this house.

LIEUTENANT PORTUONDO: Don't worry. People know who I am.

MARÍA CELIA: I'd be careful if I were you. It's not five o'clock in the afternoon.

LIEUTENANT PORTUONDO: Well, I wanted to see you, and that's all that matters. I'd like to get to know the two of you. I'd like for us to talk.

MARÍA CELIA: Talk about what, Lieutenant?

LIEUTENANT PORTUONDO: I mean talk.

MARÍA CELIA: We are talking, aren't we?

LIEUTENANT PORTUONDO: No, I mean . . . When are you going to trust me?

MARÍA CELIA: Trust you how, Lieutenant?

LIEUTENANT PORTUONDO: How can I make you stop seeing me as the enemy?

MARÍA CELIA: Being the enemy is not necessarily a bad thing. You probably know that more than I do. Lets you keep your resistance, your perspective in life.

LIEUTENANT PORTUONDO: And what's your perspective in life? How do you know it's any different than mine?

MARÍA CELIA: Oh, come on, Lieutenant.

LIEUTENANT PORTUONDO: That isn't fair . . . you hardly know me.

SOFIA: I'm going upstairs to the roof . . . it seems like there are people dancing in the streets. I want to watch them from up there.

LIEUTENANT PORTUONDO: Have another drink with us?

SOFIA: No, you'll have to excuse me.

(Sofia exits.)

LIEUTENANT PORTUONDO *(Pouring more rum in María Celia's glass)*: A little more rum. *(Refilling his glass)* Salud.

(He raises his glass. She doesn't toast, but stares him in the face. He smiles and drinks. He's amused by her control.)

You know, the more I get to know you, the more I understand your husband's letters.

MARÍA CELIA: What do you mean?

LIEUTENANT PORTUONDO: This man would do anything to have you by his side. It's all here, in this letter.

MARÍA CELIA: Do you always carry my husband's letters with you?

LIEUTENANT PORTUONDO: No. I brought you this letter tonight, because I thought you'd like to know about your husband's trip to Sweden.

MARÍA CELIA: What about his trip?

LIEUTENANT PORTUONDO: I don't know. These lines may lend themselves to more than one interpretation, and you know very well what I mean. He talks about the photos he took in Sweden. Something about them looking sad and gray. What do you think that means?

MARÍA CELIA: I don't know. They say those Northern countries look sad and melancholy.

LIEUTENANT PORTUONDO: Are you sure that doesn't mean something else? He writes about several objects he bought on his trip. They seemed to have gotten lost in the mail . . . a painting, an old book on butterflies. Could this mean that he's not having any luck getting you out of this place? Was he trying to find you an asylum in Sweden?

MARÍA CELIA: What are you after, Lieutenant? What do you want to know?! Just tell me. I mean, I'm standing here listening to you and I'm thinking, is this a new game? . . . Is it really his letter? Or is this some kind of new trial I'm supposed to endure?

LIEUTENANT PORTUONDO: Look, you can see for yourself. It's his handwriting.

(He shows her the letter, then folds it and places it back in his pocket. Silence. A part of her seems to have left the room. She walks away from him. There are tears in her eyes.)

MARÍA CELIA: You should go, Lieutenant.

LIEUTENANT PORTUONDO: I'm sorry.

MARÍA CELIA: Just go, please.

LIEUTENANT PORTUONDO: I want to try to help you, María Celia. Why won't you let me help you?

MARÍA CELIA: What can you do? We both know what that letter is saying. You know everything about my life. That was my last hope.

(Her mind is somewhere else. But she takes refuge in the absurdity of the whole thing; with a faint smile:)

Well, what would Sofie and I do in Sweden. We would probably look like two out-of-season tropical palms.

LIEUTENANT PORTUONDO: I don't think you should leave the country once you're released from this house.

MARÍA CELIA: I never thought exile was the answer. But what would I do here?

LIEUTENANT PORTUONDO: You are needed here, and I don't tell you this because you are standing in front of me and I have a couple of drinks in my head . . . Look, I'm all for change, just like you . . . That manifesto you wrote about Perestroika . . .

MARÍA CELIA: It got me nowhere, Lieutenant!

LIEUTENANT PORTUONDO: It just wasn't the right time. But now . . . Look, the island is going to open up soon, just like the rest of the world . . . Things are going to change . . .

MARÍA CELIA: Please, I prefer . . .

LIEUTENANT PORTUONDO: No, listen to me . . .

MARÍA CELIA: I prefer not to talk about it . . . All I did was write the words "change" . . . "individual rights" . . . "a little more freedom" on a piece of paper and what happened?! All my writing became suspicious, a mob threw rocks at my door, two years in prison, and then I got locked up in my own house. So please just—

LIEUTENANT PORTUONDO: I believe in what you wrote, María Celia. I'm with you . . .

(Pause.)

You know, tonight I came here wanting—I was hoping for some kind of understanding between the two of us. You and I . . . We treat each other . . .

MARÍA CELIA: I think I stopped trying to understand many things . . .

LIEUTENANT PORTUONDO: And so have I. I certainly don't try to understand why I'm here in this house. Why I'm willing to read you these letters. I gave up trying to understand. You know very well I'm risking my skin. *(For the first time he realizes this is a political confession and also a confession of the heart)*

(Sofia comes down from the roof. She stays at a distance to listen to the conversation.)

I'd like to help you stop waiting.

(Pause. She looks at him.)

MARÍA CELIA: I love my husband, Lieutenant.

LIEUTENANT PORTUONDO: I know. And I love that about you. That's how I met you. I love everything about you . . . your writing . . . your mind . . . the way you think . . . how you see the world.

SOFIA: If you're leaving, Lieutenant, you should go out the back door. The head of the neighborhood committee is sitting on her doorstep.

LIEUTENANT PORTUONDO: That's all right, compañera. Thank you. Would you give me the radio before I go? I'd like to fix it for you.

47

SOFIA: If you insist. *(Hands him the radio)*

LIEUTENANT PORTUONDO: Have a good night.

MARÍA CELIA: Lieutenant . . .

LIEUTENANT PORTUONDO: Yes . . .

MARÍA CELIA: Bring me a letter tomorrow and I want you to read me the whole thing. We'll go ahead with our arrangement.

LIEUTENANT PORTUONDO: Tomorrow then.

(He exits.)

MARÍA CELIA: Are you all right? You've been up and down the roof the whole night.

SOFIA: I walked all the way past Tito's house on top of the roof. I want to go out. I can't stand it here anymore. I just want out.

(The sound of drums fills the stage. The lights fade to black.)

Scene 2

HER HUSBAND'S LETTER FOR A STORY

The lights start to slowly come up. Sofia enters with betel palm trees in terra-cotta containers.

SOFIA: Where do you want me to put these?

MARÍA CELIA *(Offstage)*: By the doorway.

SOFIA: What's gotten into you today?

MARÍA CELIA *(Offstage)*: We need some life in this house.

SOFIA: It would take more than these shrubs.

MARÍA CELIA *(Offstage)*: Do they look good there?

SOFIA: No. They look better next to the piano.

(María Celia enters with another plant. Sofia walks to the wall and presses her ear to listen. María Celia exits and returns with another palm tree and places it by the doorway.)

We haven't heard the man next door in more than two weeks. Not a sound from in there. You think something happened to him?

MARÍA CELIA: He's probably busy working.

SOFIA: I miss listening to him. He's never been gone for so long. Maybe he's sick in the hospital.

MARÍA CELIA: Ay, Sofia . . . Why would he be in the hospital? He's strong as a horse.

SOFIA: You're right, he's strong. He's built like a bull.

MARÍA CELIA: Help me bring in the other pots.

SOFIA: I suppose the lieutenant will be coming this afternoon.

MARÍA CELIA: I suppose he will.

SOFIA: And you'll want me to sit here.

MARÍA CELIA: I was hoping you would.

SOFIA: "I was hoping," she says. I might as well be another plant in the room.

MARÍA CELIA: I'll bring in the other plants.

(She exits.)

SOFIA: That's fine. I'll do whatever you want me to do. Like always, until doomsday.

(There's a knock at the door.)

Oh God! It's probably him.

(She goes to open the door. Lieutenant Portuondo comes in.)

We weren't expecting you until much later.

LIEUTENANT PORTUONDO: Left work early today.

SOFIA: María Celia is out in the patio. This is her new plan for today, to fill the house with plants.

LIEUTENANT PORTUONDO: It looks good.

SOFIA: You think so? I can't even tell the difference. Everything looks the same to me in this place. Can I get you anything, Lieutenant?

LIEUTENANT PORTUONDO: No, thank you.

SOFIA: How are things out there in the world?

LIEUTENANT PORTUONDO: It's hot. The streets are burning from this heat.

SOFIA: Not any hotter than in this house. Have you been to the movies lately?

LIEUTENANT PORTUONDO: No, I haven't.

SOFIA: I used to love going to the movies, especially in the summer. It's a good place to escape the heat.

LIEUTENANT PORTUONDO: Yes, it is.

SOFIA: Oh, I wish you could get us a permit, Lieutenant.

LIEUTENANT PORTUONDO: What kind of permit do you want?

SOFIA: Something to go out of the house, even if it's just once a week.

MARÍA CELIA (Entering with another plant): I think this bromeliad will look nice inside the house. (Notices Lieutenant Portuondo)

SOFIA: I was just about to call you . . .

MARÍA CELIA: Hello, Lieutenant!

LIEUTENANT PORTUONDO: Hello.

SOFIA: Give me the plant, I'll put it on the table. Sit here on the sofa, Lieutenant. I think I'd rather sit by the piano.

LIEUTENANT PORTUONDO (To Sofia): I imagine this is like the old days, when your friends used to gather here to read stories and poems.

SOFIA: No, it's not the same.

LIEUTENANT PORTUONDO: I'm sure there were more people and it was livelier.

SOFIA: Many more. This place was full of life before. Now everything has a sad stare . . . Every piece of furniture has a tag like an agony. Sometimes I think I'm going to go mad in this closed-up house. I spend so much time in this damned place.

MARÍA CELIA: Well, perhaps we should start now, Sofie. *(Turns to Lieutenant Portuondo)* Lieutenant.

LIEUTENANT PORTUONDO *(Takes out a letter and begins to read)*: "My dear María Celia, Your letter came yesterday and brought with it a garden of palm trees, the wind from your patio. The little place where you sit on the roof. Sometimes I can see you without seeing you, as if I were there next to you. I can picture what you do in the morning, at what time you have coffee, comb your hair, at what time you wash your face and undress." *(He looks at her)* "Every day I dream about you, my love. I can feel your arms and legs wrapped around my body like before . . . your skin soft, delicate, tender and hot . . . your face madly alive when I am inside you . . . your voice calling out, asking me to go further . . . to go as far as death . . . I'm holding your last letter in my hands now . . . Tonight I'll sleep inside you, my love. Please write to me soon, Antonio. P.S. I'm including a few jasmine flowers from the tree outside my window. They remind me of you."

MARÍA CELIA: May I see the flowers?

(Lieutenant Portuondo gives her the three little dry flowers. She smells them. He looks at her. Silence.)

SOFIA: I . . . I feel . . . I feel as if I should do something. Maybe have something to read. So quiet all of a sudden. Maybe I could play the piano.

LIEUTENANT PORTUONDO: Yes. Play something.

SOFIA: How about this? You know this song?

(She begins to play something like "Yo te Quiero Siempre" by Lecuona. Lieutenant Portuondo walks toward the piano. He leaves the letter with María Celia. She's reading it now as she smells the flowers. Sofia immerses herself in her music. She looks at Lieutenant Portuondo as she plays. He stares at María Celia. Sofia turns her face to María Celia as she plays, then back to Lieutenant Portuondo. He lets himself be taken by the music, but his eyes always return to María Celia. Holding the flowers, María Celia walks to look at the light entering from a window. Lieutenant Portuondo watches her. Sofia closes her eyes, recoiling in the music. Lieutenant Portuondo walks toward María Celia. She is smelling the flowers, then hands them for him to smell. Sofia closes the piano and walks out of the room. María Celia and Lieutenant Portuondo turn toward Sofia. María Celia is about to go after her . . .)

LIEUTENANT PORTUONDO: Don't go . . .

(María Celia remains still, looking in the direction of her sister. Lieutenant Portuondo comes closer to her. He touches her shoulder. He kisses her neck. He turns her face. He kisses her lips, her face and all over her neck and shoulders. He makes his way down her body. He's down on his knees now kissing her legs, pulling up her dress. Her back arches, then bends forward to him as if succumbing to the pull of pleasure. The two bodies have become one on the floor. The sound of nightfall drowns the whole moment into a gentle darkness. Then full darkness.

When the lights come up again, María Celia is lying on the floor with Lieutenant Portuondo, telling him the story.)

MARÍA CELIA: Then she moves around the room, like the light that enters slowly from the lighthouse. She changes the conversation. And slowly like the high tide that creeps in the afternoon, she brings the calm sea to the room. The whole room drowns in a blue glory. He no longer remembers the marine reports. He can only smell the wet air of the bay. His whole body becomes a vessel, a galleon. His open shirt, a flying sail in the wind navigating towards her open sea.

(Sofia enters but stays at a distance, watching.)

LIEUTENANT PORTUONDO: So the woman in your story is responsible for the stolen boats. She distracts the man while she's upstairs in the tower. Does the woman love this man?

MARÍA CELIA: I think she does. But she probably doesn't want to know this.

LIEUTENANT PORTUONDO: Is that why she's lying to him?

MARÍA CELIA: Perhaps he's been lying, too. Maybe he knew the boats were being stolen all along, but he pretended not to know.

LIEUTENANT PORTUONDO: Why would he do that?

MARÍA CELIA: So she could always come back to him.

(They kiss.)

LIEUTENANT PORTUONDO: You're beautiful beyond anything I've seen in my life . . .

MARÍA CELIA: I am? Tell me that again.

LIEUTENANT PORTUONDO: You're beautiful, beautiful, beautiful . . .

MARÍA CELIA: You have awakened a hunger in me that starts from my feet to my hair, as if my mouth is once again my own, my breathing . . . like I'm tasting everything for the first time.

LIEUTENANT PORTUONDO: I want to know everything about you. I want to eat with you and shower with you . . .

MARÍA CELIA: Are you as hungry as I am?

LIEUTENANT PORTUONDO: Yes, for you.

(He kisses her neck.)

MARÍA CELIA: No, wait. I think there's some mangoes left in the kitchen.

LIEUTENANT PORTUONDO: Messy fruit, the mango.

MARÍA CELIA: Messy like you.

LIEUTENANT PORTUONDO: Let's eat it naked in your room.

(*María Celia takes him by the hand. They exit into her room. The sounds of the night fill the stage. The lights become darker. The scene moves deeper into the night as time passes.*

Sofia is restless. It's been a long night, full of a wakeful dream in which she sees herself escaping the house. She enters the living room like a shadow. She walks cautiously, holding a bundle of men's clothes. She wears a fedora. She drops the bundle of clothes on top of the sofa as she glances toward her sister's room. She listens for any sounds coming from there. She stands by the sofa and starts to disguise herself as a man, putting on a pair of pants and shirt, tucking her dress inside the pants. María Celia enters.)

MARÍA CELIA: Who's there? Who's there?

SOFIA (*In a low voice*): Shshhhhh . . . Don't scream . . . don't be frightened it's me.

MARÍA CELIA: Oh my God . . . You gave me a fright. I was . . . I thought someone . . . I thought someone had gotten in . . .

SOFIA: Shsssh . . . Go back to bed, it's still dark.

MARÍA CELIA: What are you doing?

SOFIA: I couldn't sleep.

MARÍA CELIA: Why are you dressing like a man?

SOFIA: I'm trying on Papi's clothes.

MARÍA CELIA: What do you mean you're trying on Papi's clothes? Were you going out?

SOFIA: No.

MARÍA CELIA: You're lying.

LIEUTENANT PORTUONDO (*Offstage*): María Celia . . .

MARÍA CELIA *(In a loud voice)*: Coming . . . *(To Sofia)* Take off those clothes!

SOFIA: No.

MARÍA CELIA *(Starts taking off Sofia's shirt)*: Are you crazy?

SOFIA *(Pulling away)*: I don't care what you say. I'm going out.

MARÍA CELIA: If you get caught you're going back to prison.

(Lieutenant Portuondo enters the room, but stays at a distance, watching.)

SOFIA: The hell with you. Let go.

(María Celia lets go of her arm. Sofia takes a jacket and the hat and runs off out of the house.)

MARÍA CELIA *(In a low voice)*: Sofia . . . Sofia . . .

LIEUTENANT PORTUONDO: María Celia . . .

(María Celia stays motionless. Pause. She turns to him.)

MARÍA CELIA: Would you keep this between us? —Please, Alejandro, would you do that for me?

(He looks at her, then exits into her room. María Celia remains alone. The lights fade to black.)

Scene 3

COUNTING THE LOST STITCHES

The morning after Sofia's escape. María Celia and Sofia have been arguing. Lieutenant Portuondo enters from the bedroom, holding his shirt.

LIEUTENANT PORTUONDO: Did anybody follow you?

SOFIA: I already told you. No . . . no.

LIEUTENANT PORTUONDO: Did you go into anyone's house?

SOFIA: No.

LIEUTENANT PORTUONDO: Where did you go then? Where?

SOFIA: I ran through the streets like a wild horse.

LIEUTENANT PORTUONDO: That's not what I asked you.

SOFIA: Then what do you want to know?

LIEUTENANT PORTUONDO: Did you talk to anybody?

SOFIA: Yes, I talked to the sea, to the sky, to the cars and bicycles passing me by . . . Is that what you want to know? Now leave me in peace!

LIEUTENANT PORTUONDO (*Completely enraged*): Leave you in peace! Do you know what the fuck you did!

SOFIA (*Erupting*): I know what I did and I don't need to be reminded! So you can stop looking at me as if I committed murder, because I'm not taking it back. If you're so interested . . . if you want to know what really happened to me out there, I had a good time! I sat by the seawall, felt the fresh air in my lungs. I watched people sitting in the park. A man came to me and said, "What a beautiful night." Felt like a human being again!

LIEUTENANT PORTUONDO (*To María Celia*): You know, I've about had it . . . You deal with your sister. I'm scared of what she might do next.

(*He exits into the bedroom to get the rest of his clothes. Silence.*)

SOFIA: María Celia. (*Silence. Then almost in a hush*) Look at me . . . I have to talk to you . . . Something big has happened in Russia . . . We have to talk . . .

MARÍA CELIA: Talk. After what you did, do you expect me to talk to you?

SOFIA: Listen to me . . .

MARÍA CELIA: It's bad enough being stuck in this house with your foolish self!

SOFIA: And do you think I like being stuck in here with you?

MARÍA CELIA: At least I don't do anything to jeopardize you.

SOFIA: Jeopardize me? You have him stay in here, and that's not putting me at risk . . .

(Lieutenant Portuondo storms in.)

LIEUTENANT PORTUONDO: Why don't you keep your mouth shut, when you've got nothing to say.

SOFIA: Bullshit, and you both know it! It sickens me to look at the two of you.

LIEUTENANT PORTUONDO: You walked out of this house, you piece—!

SOFIA: Oh, don't try to give me a guilty conscience! It's because of people like you . . . It's because of her that I spent two years in prison . . . her rotten books . . . her friends and their literary meetings . . . That damn letter they wrote about Perestroika . . .

MARÍA CELIA: You were the first to sign the letter. *(To Lieutenant Portuondo)* She was the first to play music at the literary meetings, when Oscarito read his poems. That scoundrel she was in love with.

SOFIA: Hah! I should've left with him to Spain. *(Turning to Lieutenant Portuondo)* He was a real man . . . Don't I wish that I had him back in my life! Him and all the other men that came my way.

MARÍA CELIA *(To Sofia)*: He was an opportunist—who went off to Europe, spouting information in all the papers about the two of us in prison. He got himself a job!

SOFIA *(To María Celia)*: He was trying to get us amnesty.

MARÍA CELIA: What amnesty? I don't see any amnesty.

SOFIA: At least he tried helping us. Not like him, who hasn't done anything to get us out.

LIEUTENANT PORTUONDO *(Enraged)*: You know I should cut off your tongue!

SOFIA *(Pushes him)*: Yes, kill me! Go ahead. I wish you would.

MARÍA CELIA *(Pulls her away)*: Sofia, stop!

(Pause.)

LIEUTENANT PORTUONDO: You don't know what the fuck you've done!

(He storms out. Silence.)

MARÍA CELIA *(Starts to knit)*: All your life begrudging me something.

SOFIA: Begrudging you what?! Why would I be jealous of you? Maybe your lieutenant is making it harder for us to get out.

(María Celia doesn't respond.)

Knit and purl, knit and purl . . . I hate those stupid needles!

(Sofia takes her needles and throws them on the floor.)

MARÍA CELIA: Pick them up . . .

(Sofia stays motionless.)

You act like a child, rash and reckless . . .

(María Celia goes to pick up the needles.)

If there's one thing we can learn from all this knitting, it's that you have to go back where you left off . . . you have to pick up the lost stitches.

SOFIA: I've lost a whole life of stitches in this house. A whole life. That's what gets to me. So many days, gone . . . I could knit a bedspread for this whole island with all the lost days. I can't even remember where I left off living my own life. My own place in this mess! I'll never forget that day when Papi left the country. When he kissed us on the forehead and told us not to fall in love, not to get married, because he was going to send for us . . . as if love was a car one could stop with the touch of the brakes. For me time stopped. I felt my feet stop growing, my bones, my breasts, as if I had frozen in time, because I was saving myself for North America. It just feels like all my life I've been waiting and I haven't lived. You got to travel with your books. You got married, when you got tired of waiting. But me, stuck here. Stuck, piano lessons, a few students, taking care of Mamá. Stuck . . . stuck . . . stuck . . . and now stuck even more.

MARÍA CELIA: Sofie please . . .

(María Celia holds on to Sofia, trying to console her.)

SOFIA: No. Can't you see what you are doing?! Can't you see what you're getting yourself into with that man? He's not going to make it better for us. I've watched him . . . He got rid of all the inspectors who used to come to this house. He's the only one who comes here. Can't you see it spelled out on his forehead. Ownership! Everything about him screams out zookeeper.

MARÍA CELIA: That's enough, Sofia! That's enough!

(There is a pause. Sofia looks at her a moment. María Celia is shaken by what Sofia has said.)

SOFIA: Last night I heard a group of men talking about Russia. Something big has happened there, María Celia. They said the Soviet Union has broken apart, that it's over . . . Can you believe it! Thousands of people in the squares . . . That's what I heard . . . All over Moscow celebrating . . . statues tumbling down . . .

(María Celia walks away. She seems to be somewhere else, lost.)

Maybe something will happen here, too.

MARÍA CELIA: Maybe.

SOFIA: One man was even talking about the new maps . . . He was saying the world is going to seem bigger with all the changes. Can you imagine? Someone is out there sketching new maps of the world.

(The lights fade to black.)

Scene 4

AFTER THE SOVIET COUP

The lights slowly come up on Sofia and Lieutenant Portuondo standing by the doorway.

LIEUTENANT PORTUONDO: Where's your sister? Did you tell her I came by earlier?

SOFIA: I did.

LIEUTENANT PORTUONDO: Did you tell her I wanted to talk to her?

SOFIA: I did. She said that she didn't think she'd be able to get up from bed. You look a little sick, too, Lieutenant. You haven't been sleeping well?

LIEUTENANT PORTUONDO: No.

SOFIA: Me neither. The summer heat is agonizing, isn't it?

LIEUTENANT PORTUONDO: Can I get your sister something?

SOFIA: She'll be fine. You must have a lot of work, Lieutenant . . . I mean, with everything that happened in Russia, you must be busy . . .

LIEUTENANT PORTUONDO: What about Russia?

SOFIA: I mean . . . So much has happened out there in the world. I mean the big revolt in Moscow . . . When I heard about it, I thought—

LIEUTENANT PORTUONDO: I'd like to talk to your sister. Why don't you call her?

SOFIA: I told you she's—

LIEUTENANT PORTUONDO: Call her! *(In a loud voice)* María Celia! *(To Sofia)* Go get her.

SOFIA: I told you she's not feeling well.

LIEUTENANT PORTUONDO: Go get her I said! *(Calling)* María Celia!

(Sofia exits, then returns.)

Is she coming?

SOFIA: I suppose so. She's up on the roof.

(María Celia enters.)

LIEUTENANT PORTUONDO: What's the matter with you?

MARÍA CELIA: Sofie must have told you, I haven't been feeling well.

LIEUTENANT PORTUONDO: Sick? and you were up on the roof.

SOFIA: She needed some air.

LIEUTENANT PORTUONDO: Is it possible to have a word with you?

(Sofia exits. He looks at María Celia.)

For three days I've been coming here. I thought you didn't want to see me.

MARÍA CELIA: Sofie told you—I haven't been feeling—

LIEUTENANT PORTUONDO: Do you need anything?

MARÍA CELIA: No, thank you.

(She moves away from him.)

LIEUTENANT PORTUONDO: Are you feeling better?

MARÍA CELIA: No.

LIEUTENANT PORTUONDO: If you like, I can go and come back later.

(Pause.)

MARÍA CELIA: Did you fix my radio?

LIEUTENANT PORTUONDO: I haven't had time to go by the shop and pick it up.

MARÍA CELIA: Would you get it for me?

LIEUTENANT PORTUONDO: Sure. I can pick it up tomorrow.

MARÍA CELIA: It seems like the whole world is upside down.

LIEUTENANT PORTUONDO: Why do you say that?

MARÍA CELIA: I can see the people from the roof. I can see through their faces . . . their eyes elsewhere . . . their minds wondering, questioning what happened in Russia.

LIEUTENANT PORTUONDO: This morning we had to arrest a boy.

MARÍA CELIA: What did he do?

LIEUTENANT PORTUONDO: He was protesting . . . he climbed to the top of a street lamp. We couldn't get him to come down. He said he was going to electrocute himself. The crowd went wild. I couldn't do anything about it. *(Shakes his head)* It was awful. He was just a boy, eleven or twelve.

MARÍA CELIA: Do you realize that boy could've been me, my sister . . . even you?

LIEUTENANT PORTUONDO: Look, it was hard enough . . . Do you think it was easy for me to arrest him? I wanted the whole thing to go away . . . but what could I do?

MARÍA CELIA: You could've let him go. He was just a boy.

LIEUTENANT PORTUONDO: I guess you don't understand my position.

MARÍA CELIA: No, I think I do. It seems like outside of these walls I wouldn't recognize you. I don't really know who you are.

LIEUTENANT PORTUONDO: Don't say that . . .

MARÍA CELIA: Even the other night when you spoke about changes, ideas, it was foolish talk.

LIEUTENANT PORTUONDO: Come here, María Celia . . .

(He takes hold of her.)

MARÍA CELIA: I think we should stop all of this.

LIEUTENANT PORTUONDO: Then what happened to the other night when you were open to me, full of arms? . . . When you took me to the patio and showed me that plant growing out of the wall . . . *(Pause)* Tell me . . .

MARÍA CELIA: I remember what I said. It's growing out of nothing with barely any soil, like us. *(Looks into the distance)*

LIEUTENANT PORTUONDO: Then what did it mean?

(She looks at him. She doesn't know what to say. She turns away, wanting this moment to disappear.)

MARÍA CELIA: When you came into this house, it seemed like everything became unknowable, unrecognizable, as if someone had robbed me of reason. There were no questions of where things might end up. I was only sure of one thing . . .

LIEUTENANT PORTUONDO: Of what?

(María Celia is silent.)

Look at me. I would have liked so many things. We had escaped this place, María Celia. We were one night ahead of the world.

MARÍA CELIA: Do you really believe it's that easy?

LIEUTENANT PORTUONDO: What are you afraid of?

MARÍA CELIA: I'm afraid of what locked-up places breed.

LIEUTENANT PORTUONDO: And what is that?

MARÍA CELIA: I think everything has been defined for us. I'm locked up in here and you're out there, and we should keep it that way.

LIEUTENANT PORTUONDO: You're trying to run so fast from me you don't even know where you're going.

MARÍA CELIA: No. I've been closed up in this house for a long time. Too long. It does something to your mind. A sort of blindness, that makes you close your eyes and see somebody else who's not there in front of you . . .

LIEUTENANT PORTUONDO: And who's that? Your husband. You see your husband in me.

MARÍA CELIA: No. It's wrong. It's all wrong . . . It's a crime . . . the same corruption that goes on out there, people bargaining for food, for a bar of soap . . . except you've been bargaining with my life . . .

LIEUTENANT PORTUONDO: We're beyond all that, María Celia.

MARÍA CELIA: Something is going to happen in this country soon. I can feel it coming like a storm.

LIEUTENANT PORTUONDO: What? The ringing of the bells, people dancing in the streets, celebrating nothing. Is that what you expect? Did you see the line of cars in front of the gasoline station?! Did you see how it extends for blocks? That's what's happening here. That's what people are talking about. The dregs the Russians left behind. The whole mess . . . Look I don't want to talk about this . . .

MARÍA CELIA: It's what I'm holding on to.

LIEUTENANT PORTUONDO (Enraged): You know I'm tired of hearing about the fuckin' Russians! Who cares what happened in Russia! Who the fuck cares, goddamn it!

MARÍA CELIA: I think you should leave, Lieutenant.

LIEUTENANT PORTUONDO: Oh, no . . . I'm staying right here. I'm not going anywhere. I'm not going anywhere. (*Pacing back and forth)* It's strange this thing you have over me. The worst of it is you can't make it stop, and I can't do anything about it. I've always been a clean revolutionary—as clean as can be. Not one stain on my record. You came into my life and you got inside me like a war. I don't even recognize myself. I can't even think straight anymore. You know very well I've been throwing my life away because of you, and I have far more to lose than you do.

MARÍA CELIA: Do you really think this can go anywhere?

LIEUTENANT PORTUONDO: Why not?

MARÍA CELIA: Yes the two of us like outlaws, criminals of some kind ... There's another side to me ... something you don't want to face ... I carry a whole past behind me ... a whole past ...

LIEUTENANT PORTUONDO: You're talking as if I didn't—

MARÍA CELIA: No! You can never put yourself in my place! I made certain decisions long ago, which have locked me up in here.

LIEUTENANT PORTUONDO: Look, I've been talking to the high officials ... I've been trying to get you out.

MARÍA CELIA: I don't want any help. If I'm not out of this house anytime soon, I'm going on a hunger strike.

LIEUTENANT PORTUONDO: A hunger strike? And what are you going to get out of it?

(Sofia enters.)

Have you considered well what's happening out there? I suppose you don't realize what's going on. As we speak, brigades are being formed everywhere on the island, to crack down any rebellion or demonstrations ...

MARÍA CELIA: That's not going to stop me. I want to change like the rest of the world.

LIEUTENANT PORTUONDO: You try to do your silly strike and the two of you will go back to point zero.

MARÍA CELIA: We are at point zero, Lieutenant.

LIEUTENANT PORTUONDO: I warn you. You try and do anything, and you'll have a mob storming into this house to force-feed you . . . And not with food but with every one of your books.

MARÍA CELIA: You don't frighten me, Lieutenant. You use the power that's been given to you foolishly. You persecute people like me . . . you pry . . . you investigate my life, because you don't know what to do with yourself . . . You don't know what to do with your own existence which amounts to nothing!

SOFIA: You should leave, Lieutenant. Please, just go . . . just go.

LIEUTENANT PORTUONDO: Ask your sister if she has anything else to say.

(Silence.)

You want change? Then things will change!

(Lieutenant Portuondo looks at María Celia a moment, then makes his way out of the room, slamming the door behind him. Sofia turns to her sister. María Celia crosses to the piano. The lights fade to black.)

EPILOGUE

Twining Our Lives

The piano has been taken away. The house looks very empty. Sofia sits on a chair where the piano used to be. She looks into the distance. María Celia twines yarn as she recites a letter to her husband.

MARÍA CELIA: "It is late at night now and I strain my eyes to see your face. This morning I opened the door of the wardrobe and hugged your black suit which hangs next to my clothes. Here nothing has changed, my love. If anything, the regime has reduced the distribution of food once again. As for clothing supplies each person can expect a dress or a pair of pants every two years. Sofie hasn't been doing well. Yesterday the only joy and little amusement we had, was taken away from us. A group of men came to our house to take Sofie's piano away."

(Sofia walks to the wall. She presses her ear against the concrete partition.)

"We've started a little protest on our roof and a hunger strike. For the time being we wait. This year the guava tree in our patio has given so much fruit, we don't know what to do with all the guavas. And since Sofie and I are not eating, and the neighbors won't accept anything from us, we bring the fruit into the house and put them everywhere, because the fragrance of the guava reminds us of Grandma Carucha and Mami. It's like an invisible woman with a sweet perfume is staying with us, and the house feels less empty."

(Sofia now looks as if she has lost her mind.)

SOFIA: María Celia, I think he's home. Come here. I thought I heard him. Do you hear anything?

MARÍA CELIA: I don't hear a thing.

SOFIA: Shshh . . . Come close to the wall. You hear his footsteps? He's come back.

(María Celia goes along with what her sister is hearing, a way of consoling her.)

MARÍA CELIA: Yes. I can hear him.

SOFIA: You think he's alone?

MARÍA CELIA: No.

SOFIA: Did you hear other footsteps? He's standing still.

MARÍA CELIA: I think he's drinking.

SOFIA: Already.

MARÍA CELIA: He must drink to forget. The pangs of love, Sofie.

SOFIA: María Celia, I used to play that song on the piano. You remember? He's playing that song in his house. What should I do María Celia? What should I do?

MARÍA CELIA: Just listen, Sofie. Be still and listen.

(Soft piano music is heard through the wall. The music plays louder.
Lieutenant Portuondo knocks on the door.)

Just listen to the music . . . just listen . . .

(The music swells. The sisters let themselves be taken by the music, disregarding the knocking at the door. The music continues to swell, drowning out the persistent knocking. Blackout.)

END OF PLAY

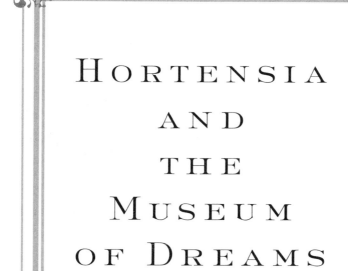

Hortensia
and
the
Museum
of Dreams

Hortensia and the Museum of Dreams was commissioned by the
Latino Theatre Initiative at Center Theatre Group's Mark Taper
Forum in Los Angeles, California. *Hortensia and the Museum of
Dreams* premiered September 15, 2001, at the New Theatre (Rafael
de Acha, Artistic Director; Eileen Suarez, Managing Director) in
Coral Gables, Florida. It was directed by Rafael de Acha; the set
design was by Michelle Cumming, the lighting design was by Travis
Neff, the sound design was by Steve Shapiro; the production
stage manager was Amanda Lee Clark. The cast was as follows:

LUCIANA	Tanya Bravo
LUCA	Carlos Orizondo
HORTENSIA/MAMÁ FEFA	Marta Velasco
SAMUEL/OFFICER	Robert Maxwell
BASILIO/OFFICER	David Perez-Ribada
GENERAL VIAMONTE/FAUSTINO/	
TIO LALO/GUSTAVO SOTO/	
HEREDIA	Ramon Gonzalez-Cuevas
DELITA/HOTEL RECEPTIONIST/	
AMPARO DE LAS ROSAS/	
ABELARDA/MERCEDITA PEREZ	Ursula Freundlich

CHARACTERS

LUCIANA, a woman in her thirties (she's older in real life)

LUCA, Luciana's brother, thirties (he's older in real life)

HORTENSIA, mother of Samuel and Basilio, early fifties

SAMUEL, Basilio's brother, early twenties

BASILIO, Samuel's brother, twenties

GENERAL VIAMONTE, works for the Interior Ministry, forties

DELITA, a woman in her twenties

Note: Luciana and Luca should look younger than their actual age, as if their lost childhood has stopped them from aging.

OTHER CHARACTERS:

MAMÁ FEFA (played by the actor playing Hortensia)

OFFICER 1 (played by the actor playing Samuel)

OFFICER 2 (played by the actor playing Basilio)

FAUSTINO, TIO LALO, GUSTAVO SOTO
(played by the actor playing General Viamonte)

HOTEL RECEPTIONIST, AMPARO DE LAS ROSAS, MERCEDITA PEREZ
(played by the actor playing Delita)

Cuba. The pope's visit, January 21–25, 1998.

SET

The set should have a feeling of openness. A Tibetan bell is used as a way of suspending reality.

ACT ONE

The music of an Afro-Cuban lullaby plays. In darkness we hear the sound of an airplane flying overhead. A slide of a boy and a girl holding suitcases is projected on a wall. Spotlight on Luciana and Luca, each sitting on her/his suitcase. They are in different spaces and don't relate to one another. Both hold travel journals and address the audience.

Traveling

LUCA: January 2nd: The Airport.

LUCIANA: January 2nd: The Plane.

LUCA: My mother gave me this travel journal.

LUCIANA *(Looks at the journal in her hand)*: She said write everything down.

LUCA: Write everything down, she said.

LUCIANA: Because the island will never be the same.

LUCA *(Opens the journal; laughs)*: My mother.

LUCIANA *(Holds journal close to her chest)*: My mother.

LUCA *(Looks at the journal in his hand)*: What do I do with a journal? Do I write that I don't know how to begin? Should I write that I'm looking for my sister?

LUCIANA *(Reading from her journal)*: I am a traveler about to disembark on the land I left with my brother when I was eleven.

LUCA: Should I write that I have to find my sister? Should I write that it's been so long since I saw her last?

LUCIANA: In case you find this journal, please get rid of it—throw it into the sea . . .

(Sound of a large wave drowning the scene. Airport sounds. Two men dressed in militia uniforms enter the stage. Officer 1 approaches Luca, Officer 2 approaches Luciana. The Officers face the audience.)

The Arrival

OFFICER 1: Passport, señor?

OFFICER 2: Passport, señora?

OFFICER 1: Where are you coming from?

LUCIANA 1: The U.S.

LUCA: The U.S.

OFFICER 1 *(Flips through passport pages)*: Visiting relatives?

LUCIANA: No, I am a journalist.

LUCA: Visiting relatives, Officer.

OFFICER 2: Documenting the visit of the pope?

LUCA: No.

LUCIANA: That's correct.

OFFICER 1: Where are you staying?

LUCIANA: Hotel Capri.

LUCA: Staying with relatives, Officer.

OFFICER 2: Proceed.

OFFICER 1: Proceed.

(Sound of drums.)

In the City

LUCIANA: January 2nd: Havana.

LUCA: If I close my eyes I can see it like before . . .

LUCIANA: The seawall . . .

LUCA: Same old streets.

LUCIANA: Same old blue . . .

LUCA: Same cars.

LUCIANA: Nothing like this blue.

LUCA: Just like yesterday.

LUCIANA: This is the place we went to school!

LUCA: This is the park we used to go to every afternoon!

LUCIANA: I can remember Mamá's voice the day we left . . .

(Lights up on Mamá Fefa, wearing a 1950s dress and a scarf, and holding a small red suitcase.)

MAMÁ FEFA: Never let go of your brother's hand. Hold on to your ticket. Over there you'll be in different surroundings . . . Never forget me and your father, and take care of your new shoes . . .

LUCIANA: But I didn't come here to retrace the past, I came to see the new generation . . . the new island . . .

77

A Place Called Home

Lights come up on Tio Lalo standing next to Luca. He is disheveled, wears glasses and is hard of hearing. He holds an old cigar box full of photographs.

TIO LALO: Here are some old photographs of you and your sister.

(*Lights come up on a Hotel Receptionist. She hands Luciana the key to her room.*)

HOTEL RECEPTIONIST: Here is the key to your room, señora. Here are some papers for you to sign. And I will need your passport again.

LUCIANA: My passport?

HOTEL RECEPTIONIST: Part of the procedure, señora.

TIO LALO (*To Luca*): Here's a towel and soap. It's better to bathe in the morning because the electricity is cut off after six.

HOTEL RECEPTIONIST: Here's your itinerary for tomorrow . . . Wake-up call is at eight . . . Your tour guide is Ramon.

LUCIANA: But I don't want a tour guide.

HOTEL RECEPTIONIST: It's all been arranged for your convenience, señora.

TIO LALO: Here's a bucket.

LUCA: But, Tio Lalo.

TIO LALO: If you want to bathe in the evening, you'll have to heat up water in this bucket. And if you want hot water, you have to take the bucket across the street and buy some charcoal.

LUCA: Tio Lalo.

TIO LALO: I'll go get you a pillow.

LUCIANA (*Facing the audience*): I was told about the organized tours for visitors.

LUCA (*Facing the audience*): I was told about the power outages.

LUCIANA: I wasn't going to take part in any of this.

LUCA: But a bucket of water!

LUCIANA: I never liked tours to begin with . . .

LUCA: A bucket of charcoal!

(Luciana and Luca open a couple of maps and spread them on the floor.)

Maps and the City

LUCIANA: If I make a right on N Street . . . If I walk down L Street.

LUCA: If I walk straight through La Rampa Boulevard . . .

LUCIANA: If I make a left on K Street I can cut through the park . . .

LUCA *(Folds the map)*: I'm remembering the streets . . .

LUCIANA *(Folds the map)*: The streets are remembering me . . .

LUCA: Blue skies, faded awnings, orange tiles . . .

LUCIANA: The world is not forgetful . . . A sidewalk never forgets to be a sidewalk . . . A tree never forgets to be a tree.

LUCA: If I stop at the Coppelia . . .

LUCIANA: If I stop at the university.

LUCA: No, I don't need a map . . .

(Lights come up on the Hotel Receptionist.)

HOTEL RECEPTIONIST: I'm sorry, señor, but the guest you're looking for is not in her room.

LUCA: Can I leave her a note?

HOTEL RECEPTIONIST: If you wish.

(Slide projection of a young boy holding a suitcase.)

LUCA *(Facing the audience)*: My Dear Sister, I've only been here for a day and I was wondering if it's possible to see you. After all these years we should talk again and settle the past. I'm staying at Tio Lalo's house. I must confess to you that this morning there was once again a kind of hope in me for a new beginning. I could see the two of us traveling together and visiting our old house. In some ways I was arranging all the furniture in my mind and telling them, "Sshh! Soon she'll be coming back." Love, your brother, Luca.

LUCIANA *(Astonished)*: My brother . . .

(Lights up on Mamá Fefa with the small red suitcase. Sound of an airplane. Luciana looks into the distance.)

MAMÁ FEFA *(Waving and crying out to her children)*: Never let go of your brother's hand. When you go up the stairs to the airplane, look for my polka-dotted scarf in the crowd and wave good-bye, so I know you're safe. So I know you're leaving, my love. Never let go of your brother's hand!

LUCIANA: I decide to stay in Havana for a few days.

LUCA: I try again to see her.

LUCIANA: I've been able to get away from the guided tours.

LUCA: I spend a lot of time walking through the streets trying to find her.

LUCIANA: I don't think I can face him now.

LUCA: I find myself stopping in front of houses and photographing old wooden doors. *(Takes photos)*

LUCIANA: In a secret way I'm collecting faces, streets and romantic corners . . .

LUCA: I am placing my sister's face on other women . . .

LUCIANA: A few times I've noticed that a black car is following me.

(Luca turns to Luciana. They are together.)

LUCA: Luciana! Did you get my note?

LUCIANA: What are you doing here?

LUCA: I thought it was time. We should talk.

LUCIANA: I'm here for work.

LUCA: Luciana, look at me.

LUCIANA: I can't, Luca. I can't. I have to go.

(She walks away.)

LUCA: Luciana.

(Afro-Cuban music plays.)

LUCIANA: I take a bus. I want it to take me anywhere. Somewhere far away. The streets are still dark. With the power outages, most of the city resorts to the light of the moon, and Havana looks like a sleeping madam who lost her pearl necklace.

(Slide projection of a young girl holding a suitcase.)

LUCA *(Facing the audience)*: The heat wakes me up. I leave the house early in the morning. I go to the hotel hoping to see Luciana again. I find out she has left the city. I walk and walk. I want to get lost, for the ground to swallow me. I sit by the seawall. I talk to sea. I talk to the waves.

(Sound of a large wave. Blue lights.)

Delita, Who Alleviates the Heart

Delita enters on skates. She circles Luca. She wears lots of makeup.

DELITA: If you need to be left alone, just tell me. But you look like you need some company . . .

LUCA: No. I'm just . . .

DELITA: I live around the corner. My cat, Orlando, just died. I was miserable and alone in my apartment, so I thought I should

shake off my calamity. Do you want to come up for a drink?
I have some rum and good music.

LUCA: No. I'm just . . .

DELITA: What is your name?

LUCA: Luca.

DELITA: Italiano?

LUCA: No.

DELITA: Portuguese?

LUCA: No.

DELITA: I'm Delita. Can you believe somebody gave me a canary?
Quite frankly, I thought it was bad taste, because how can
you replace a cat with a canary. So I opened the window and
let the thing fly free. Now I'm resisting going back to my
place 'cause I know I'll feel lonely without Orlando. Why
don't you come with me? I'm just around the corner. (*Takes
hold of his arm*)

LUCA: No. I'm . . .

DELITA: Come on . . .

LUCA: I have to go . . .

DELITA: I'm just around the corner.

(*He lets her guide him. They exit.*)

The Museum of Dreams

LUCIANA (*Sitting on her suitcase*): I get to a small town called
Santiago de las Vegas, I find a small hotel . . . They don't
have rooms until noon, so I roam around the town . . .

(*Samuel enters holding a machete and wearing a straw hat.*)

SAMUEL: If you're here to see my mother, you should come in the
front gate. It's not polite to wander through private prop-
erty without announcing yourself . . .

LUCIANA: I'm sorry, I didn't know . . .

SAMUEL: Have you come to see my mother?

LUCIANA: No, I was . . .

SAMUEL: She's expecting you . . .

LUCIANA: Me? No, you must . . . I was just wandering through the place . . .

SAMUEL: Spying?

LUCIANA: I saw the museum sign.

SAMUEL: Two officers were here yesterday . . . My mother was right. Nothing on this island comes in even numbers, so that makes you the third officer . . .

LUCIANA: I think you're mistaken . . . I'm not . . .

SAMUEL: Our dogs can smell a stranger from kilometers away . . .

LUCIANA: Look I'm not from here—

SAMUEL: So is the Interior Ministry sending—?

LUCIANA: I'm not from here. I'm from the United States.

SAMUEL: The United States . . .

LUCIANA: Yes . . . I'm a journalist. I'm here for the pope's visit.

SAMUEL: You are?!

(In a loud voice, starts calling his brother) Basilio . . . Basilio . . . Come fast . . . Come fast . . . She's here . . .

(To Luciana) So you've answered my mother's letters . . .

LUCIANA: Look . . . I'm afraid.

SAMUEL: Basilio, come fast . . . She's here . . .

LUCIANA: Who are you calling?

SAMUEL: My brother . . . He'll be very happy to see you . . .

(Basilio enters.)

Come close, Basilio . . . This lady . . . she's come to visit us . . . Call Mamá . . . The letters worked . . . She's here with the pope . . .

LUCIANA: Wait a minute . . . I think you're mistaken—

SAMUEL: No. This is the place—

BASILIO: Please come with us—

SAMUEL: We're not mistaken, señora . . .

BASILIO: Please, come this way. Our mother will be honored—

LUCIANA: Now wait a minute! Why are you taking me to see your mother?

BASILIO: Because it will make her very happy to know—

LUCIANA: Wait! You're confusing me.

SAMUEL: Yes, I'm sorry I confused you . . . I confused her with the militia, Basilio . . . Crazy me . . .

BASILIO (*Gives Samuel a shove*): You knucklehead . . . Bobo . . . I'm sorry he did that . . . It's just that the militia has been here a few times because of all the letters we sent abroad. We've had so many problems with the museum, you see.

SAMUEL: One officer was hollering at Mamá . . . Basilio wanted to cut off his head.

BASILIO (*Slaps Samuel gently*): You don't have to tell her that!

SAMUEL: But it's true . . . We had to put up a good fight.

BASILIO: What he's trying to say . . . We were told that the pope's tour had been organized and nobody was going to come here.

SAMUEL: We knew they were lying to us because, look, you've come—

BASILIO: They just wanted to close the museum—

SAMUEL: And if Mamá hadn't stood up to that man—

BASILIO: That's enough, Samuel! We still don't know your name . . .

LUCIANA: . . . I'm sorry, I think you're—

BASILIO: But what is your name?

LUCIANA: Luciana María.

BASILIO: Luciana . . . Sounds Spanish.

LUCIANA: I was born here.

BASILIO: You were born here? So that makes you one of us . . .

SAMUEL: And your last name?

LUCIANA: Harland. (*They react to the foreign last name*) My husband's name.

BASILIO: Luciana María Harland . . . Beautiful name . . .

SAMUEL: I'm Samuel and he's Basilio.

BASILIO: We've burdened you with our story . . .

LUCIANA: No. Not at all . . . I'm . . . *(Not finding the words)* I'm in awe.

(Both brothers look at each other and laugh at the awkwardness of the moment.)

SAMUEL: She's beautiful, isn't she?

BASILIO: Yes. Sorry we confused you.

LUCIANA: Confused is not the word. All of a sudden I don't know where I am.

BASILIO: You've come here and that's what matters. Welcome to my mother's house. Welcome to the Museum of Dreams . . .

(Sound of a large wave.)

Delita After Love

Luca and Delita. He's barefoot, wearing only a T-shirt and pants. He walks forward with a drink in his hand. Delita remains standing in the back.

DELITA: Don't leave yet.

LUCA: I have to go back to my uncle's house.

DELITA: You look sad.

LUCA: I'm not.

DELITA *(Approaches him)*: It's always like this when you do it in the afternoon. I get blue just the same. Maybe because there's too much light. Would you like me to make you some café? I always drink some after I make love, or I stand on my head. I do it to thin the blood . . . The blood gets crazy, it starts palpitating on its own, forming little hearts everywhere in the body. *(Holds him)* —You know, you never told me how old you are. Let me guess, twenty-eight. *(He shakes his head)* Thirty.

LUCA: No.

DELITA: Thirty-three.

LUCA: Sometimes I don't know how old I am.

DELITA: What do you mean?

LUCA: I don't know. I mean, my body has stopped recognizing my age.

DELITA: God, don't tell me I've slept with a vampire!

LUCA *(Laughs)*: No. A doctor told me that I suffer from an aging disorder. My sister, too.

DELITA: Is it contagious? Will it make me be young for the rest of my life?

LUCA *(Laughs)*: Maybe.

DELITA: I like it when you smile. Why don't you stay longer?

LUCA: I ought to go . . . My uncle . . .

DELITA: You look like you need to talk.

LUCA: What makes you think that?

DELITA: I know these things. I'd be dead if it wasn't for my mouth.

LUCA: So you think talking helps.

DELITA *(Nods)*: Come on, tell me. Why are you so gloomy?

LUCA: Just trying to adjust. Everybody tried to prepare me for this trip. They told me about the power being cut off, the shortage of food. How buildings are falling apart. How people live double lives.

DELITA: Is that what it is?

LUCA: Well, nobody can ever tell you how it affects you inside.

DELITA: Don't leave yet. Stay a while longer.

(Sound of a large wave. The wave takes Luca and Delita away.)

A Journal Entry

LUCA: January 8th: Later that day . . . Regret, intrigue, fear . . . Luca
in my mind. I am marking the same old maps of the past.
—No, mustn't think of these things. I've moved on . . . I
have begun traveling. Here I am deep in the island and this
museum intrigues me. Any serious traveler looks forward
to these moments when itineraries cease to exist—when
you get deliriously lost and the thrill and the fear of the
unknown take over.

Meeting Hortensia

*Samuel and Basilio have gotten their mother, Hortensia, and now the
family stands close to Luciana. The brothers have brought two chairs.*

SAMUEL: Her name is Luciana María . . . Señora Luciana María
Harland.

LUCIANA: Lucy . . . you can call me Lucy.

HORTENSIA: Ah, Lucy, better, shorter. I'm Hortensia but they call
me Horte. Good for you, too, eh! Hortensia is too long.

SAMUEL *(Still excited)*: She came from the States, Mamá, just to
see us.

LUCIANA: Your son thinks—

HORTENSIA: I knew somebody was coming, the saints told me—

LUCIANA: I should explain . . .

SAMUEL: Later, Señora Luciana . . . You can explain later . . .

LUCIANA: But you must understand . . . it was by coincidence . . .
I was walking—

HORTENSIA: There's no coincidence, Señora Luciana: Nothing is
coincidental. Look up the word "coincidence" in the dic-
tionary— "remarkable events," I think it says.

BASILIO *(Laughs)*: You were sent to us, Señora Luciana.

(Looks at his brother. They both laugh.)

LUCIANA *(Amused by Samuel's innocent laugh)*: I was!

(The brothers look at her.)

HORTENSIA: I had a dream about a woman. She looked like a foreigner with a suitcase in her hand . . . Did you tell her, Basilio? She was wearing a hat like you.

LUCIANA: Like me . . .

HORTENSIA: Yes.

LUCIANA: That's true, I'm wearing a hat.

BASILIO *(Looking at her with delight; laughs)*: Did you forget, Señora Luciana? Did you forget that you're still wearing a hat?

LUCIANA: No. No, of course not. After a while you don't sense it. *(All of a sudden she realizes they might be asking her to take off her hat)* Oh, I'm sorry I didn't take off my hat. I'm inside your house . . . I should've taken it off.

HORTENSIA: It's all right, señora. My mother would have minded, but not me. "No hats inside the house," she used to say. Samuel, get her a glass of water! *(To Luciana)* We haven't offered you anything. Please sit . . . *(To Samuel)* And make her a beautiful cup of fresh café.

LUCIANA: No, don't trouble yourself.

SAMUEL: It's no trouble, señora. *(Exits)*

HORTENSIA: I remember telling Basilio about the dream I had the night before. "Something tells me that was a message from the sky . . . A woman from a foreign country is coming and she will sit here in this room with us . . . "

LUCIANA: Is that so?

BASILIO: It never fails to happen . . . Mamá's dreams always come true.

HORTENSIA: When did you arrive in the country, Señora Luciana?

LUCIANA: Oh, about three or four days ago.

HORTENSIA: So this is the first place you visited?

LUCIANA: Practically . . .

(Samuel returns with the café. He stands close to his mother.)

HORTENSIA: Samuel was beginning to think that nobody was going to visit us from abroad.

SAMUEL: That's not true, Mamá.

HORTENSIA: I said to him, "Of course somebody is going to come. There is going to be people here from all over the world: cardinals, bishops, reporters . . . Why wouldn't they be interested in our museum . . . " They both found all these addresses at the local church, the National Something of Churches . . .

SAMUEL: National Association, Mamá . . .

HORTENSIA: That place . . . We sent letters inviting them to come here.

BASILIO: But we didn't know if they'd be interested in our museum—

HORTENSIA: The museum is not really about dreams . . . it's about miracles . . .

LUCIANA: Miracles!

SAMUEL: We called it the "Museum of Dreams" because we thought it was more appropriate.

HORTENSIA: If we were living in another place it would've been called the Museum of Miracles.

SAMUEL: Mamá didn't think the word miracle was right . . .

HORTENSIA: No. Not for this system we live in, sounded too religious.

SAMUEL: And one night it came to her, right Mamá?

HORTENSIA *(Laughs)*: Yes, the whole name . . .

SAMUEL: A wise spirit whispered the name in her ear . . . That's how it was, wasn't it?

HORTENSIA: That's right, "The Museum of Dreams," she said . . . And I thought, That's it. It sounds promising . . .

BASILIO: Revolutionary . . .

HORTENSIA: All those things we're always talking about: ideals, dreams and klin, klan: The Museum of Dreams. *(Laughs at her own inventions)* — Here one has to be inventive, Señora Luciana: If you want to survive you have to be clever and figure things out. The Africans say that turtles belong to the fire sign, like scorpions. But turtles are wise, they live in rivers so they don't burn and consume themselves.

BASILIO: Oh, Mamá there you go again with your African philosophy! What she's trying to say . . .

HORTENSIA: We are miracle collectors, Señora Luciana: We collect what's been omitted and neglected in this country. I've been collecting miracles, before these two were born. It's something that has been passed on to me.

There was a woman named Mamá Rita. She was the one who started collecting the miracles. She used to teach the poor to read and write . . .

SAMUEL: She taught Mamá to read.

HORTENSIA: She used to tell her students that once they had learned to write their blessings, they were literate. That's how the miracles started to be written and collected. The poor used to come from all over with their miracles written on little papers.

SAMUEL: And if they didn't have paper they used to write their miracles on the sleeves of old shirts . . .

HORTENSIA: Oh, they'd write their blessings on everything, dry leaves, old handkerchiefs . . . The word got around and it became a tradition. But things got ugly with the revolution, all of a sudden it was forbidden to be religious.

BASILIO: But people continued sending their miracles, Luciana . . .

HORTENSIA: For many years we wanted to build a museum. But it never seemed possible. I used to tell the boys it's not time yet . . . not the right time to open a museum . . .

SAMUEL: Until Mamá said, "Let's open it!"

(They all laugh at their courage and perseverance.)

HORTENSIA: Oh, we got complaints from the locals . . .

SAMUEL: Complaints? *(Laughs)* They wanted it closed!

HORTENSIA: They said it was fanaticism! But since the pope was coming and the whole island was pretending to be religious, I pretended to be a loon and nailed the museum sign outside.

(They all laugh.)

Will you be staying with us, Señora Luciana?

LUCIANA: No. I . . .

HORTENSIA: Please do.

LUCIANA: There's a hotel around the corner . . .

SAMUEL: We have a comfortable bed and clean sheets.

HORTENSIA: We should prepare the guest room, Samuel . . . Lucy might stay with us . . .

LUCIANA: I was thinking . . . I was going to stay in the hotel . . .

SAMUEL: What for? We have plenty of room.

BASILIO: Please, be our guest.

HORTENSIA: It will be an honor if you stay.

(Nighttime. The sound of the tropical night fills the stage. The boys are fixing Luciana's room. They bring her suitcase in and hang a hammock. Hortensia brings a kerosene lamp.)

Thinking of Him

LUCIANA: January 8th: Evening . . . Eyes open . . . Thinking about Luca again. I hear voices of birds clamoring in the distance. It's the frightening sound of falling trees. The tears of wood and leaves. My brother's eyes.

(The sound of wind and distant African drums and chanting.)

Thinking of Her

LUCA: I went back to our old house, I found you in every room. Even if you have chosen to remove yourself, you were there in the patio, in the living room, standing by the window . . . I hope you come back and we could visit the island together.

A Jar of Fireflies

Samuel, Basilio and Luciana. Samuel holds a jar full of fireflies.

SAMUEL: I was going to leave you this present in the room.
LUCIANA: What is it?
SAMUEL: Fireflies . . . *(Gives her the jar)*
LUCIANA: Fireflies!
SAMUEL: I caught them for you.
LUCIANA: For me?
SAMUEL: Yes.
LUCIANA: Thank you.

(The brothers compete in trying to charm her.)

BASILIO: They are supposed to be sacred insects. In the old days people used to say that fireflies light the road to dreams.
SAMUEL: And I read somewhere that women used to wear them in their hair like stars. I bet you'd look like a beautiful night if you wear them.
BASILIO *(Messes Samuel's hair)*: My brother . . . He has been reading too many poetry books . . .
SAMUEL: Shut up! He doesn't like me to read poetry.

LUCIANA (*Amused by the two boys*): Why not?

BASILIO: He's obsessed with writing poems on tree trunks.

SAMUEL: I noticed the books you brought. I like people who read
. . . I'd like to marry a woman who likes reading, and traveling. Someone who likes to climb mountains and trees.

BASILIO: I told him he doesn't want a wife, he wants a Girl Scout.

(*Samuel smacks him to be quiet. They both laugh from embar-
rassment.*)

SAMUEL: Shut up!

BASILIO (*Messes Samuel's hair again*): My brother has a fascina-
tion for climbing trees. Sometimes I don't know if I have a
brother or a chicken. (*Tickles him*) He likes to sleep on top
of the roof.

SAMUEL (*Hits him*): Why are you—?

LUCIANA: In Italy I used to sleep on the roof. Every night I'd fall
asleep looking at the stars.

SAMUEL (*Messes Basilio's hair*): You see I'm not that strange.
Luciana is just like me . . .

BASILIO: Come on, let's go. We're keeping her from going to bed.
(*To Luciana*) Tomorrow I'd like to take you to the springs,
if you're up for it.

SAMUEL: And the cave, Basilio. (*To Luciana*) There's a beautiful
cave I'd like to show you.

BASILIO: You think you might like to go?

LUCIANA: Yes, of course.

BASILIO: Sleep well, Señora Luciana.

SAMUEL: Don't forget to put the jar by your bed . . .

LUCIANA: Good night.

(*The brothers exit. Luciana lifts up the jar and looks at the fireflies. Then she takes off her dress. She sits in her slip by the
light of the kerosene lamp, writing.*)

Pleasure in Her Name

SAMUEL: You think it was stupid of me to give her the fireflies?

BASILIO: No. It's not as bad as giving her a frog . . .

SAMUEL: Well, I don't want her to think I'm retarded. *(Looks in her direction)* I love her . . . I love her . . .

BASILIO *(Takes off his shirt)*: Yes, you told me that already . . . I like her, too.

SAMUEL: It's a shame she's married.

BASILIO *(Uses the shirt to dry his sweat)*: It's hot. Give me a light.

(They sit on the ground smoking. Samuel takes off his shirt. They can see the light coming from her room.)

SAMUEL *(Looking in Luciana's direction)*: She must be getting ready to go to sleep now. You think she sleeps naked?

BASILIO: In this heat, probably . . .

SAMUEL: When we go to the city, I want you to take me to the whore you told me about.

BASILIO: Which one?

SAMUEL: The one who plays music in her room.

(Luciana is listening now. She is amused by their conversation and is laughing.)

Did she play music the whole night?

BASILIO: Yes, boleros . . .

SAMUEL: Was she good?

BASILIO: Like fucking a guitar . . .

SAMUEL: I've never done it to music, only to the mooing of cows and the quacking of chickens in the stable. Sometimes I can't concentrate. It's different with music, isn't it?

BASILIO: Much more . . .

SAMUEL: I bet. You can do it to the rhythm: pin . . . pan . . . poon. Does she really have men come in and out of the room the whole night?

BASILIO: Many men . . .

SAMUEL: And the music, does it ever stop?

BASILIO: No. It goes on forever . . . She uses the music to drown out the men when they cry from pleasure . . .

SAMUEL: Yeah, Melba likes to scream loud when I do it with her. She scares the cows and chickens in the stable. The whole stable gets going . . . I have to cover her mouth. It's different with whores isn't it?

BASILIO: Yes, they do anything you want.

SAMUEL: And if I want them to pretend to be Luciana María . . .

BASILIO: Ah, Luciana María . . . I get a hard-on just hearing her name . . . *(He touches himself. They both laugh)* Should we go for the old hand and think about her?

SAMUEL: If you want.

(Each covers his crotch with his shirt and unzips his pants. They begin to touch themselves.)

BASILIO: You know, they say some men go to the brothels to talk like this . . .

SAMUEL: Like confession?

BASILIO: Yes, and the women listen to their dreams . . . They come to spill their hearts out . . .

SAMUEL: I bet the woman who plays music will charge more if I talk about Luciana María.

BASILIO: Ah, that name, Luciana María . . .

SAMUEL: It must cost more when you talk about your heart. Do I just go in and tell her to be like Luciana María?

BASILIO: Ah, Luciana María . . .

SAMUEL: Answer me . . .

BASILIO: Yes, then she'll play a record to make you relax. Then she'll take your pinga in her hand and dip it in a glass of rum . . .

SAMUEL (*In shock, stops touching himself*): What do you mean she's going to put my thing in a glass of rum?

BASILIO: Yeah, in rum.

SAMUEL: What for? Why rum?

BASILIO: Alcohol . . . You know microbes, germs . . . diseases . . . she's got to disinfect it . . .

SAMUEL: But I'm . . . I've never . . . Will it sting?

BASILIO: Like fire it does. You'll like it. It'll get your pinga all fired up.

SAMUEL: Forget it. You spoiled it for me.

BASILIO (*Softly*): Ah, Luciana María . . . Luciana María . . . Luciana María . . . (*Reaches an orgasm*)

SAMUEL (*After a pause*): Did you finish?

BASILIO (*There was more*): Luciana María . . . María . . . Madre Mía . . . Madre María . . . (*He slumps down*)

(*Pause.*)

SAMUEL: I didn't. Would you help me think about her?

(*Luciana turns off her light. They look in her direction.*)

She's gone to sleep now. Would you help me see her in my mind? Would you do that for me?

(*Lights change. The sound of drums.*)

Strolling Through Havana

Luca and Tio Lalo enter talking. They stand in front of a church.

TIO LALO: This section is called the Angel's Hill. And this is the church where you and your sister were baptized.

LUCA: Is this the same place where the parents would come and sign off the children?

TIO LALO: What children?

LUCA: You know, all the kids that were sent to America. The Pedro Pan kids, like me and my sister.

TIO LALO: I don't know. I didn't take part in any of that. I was opposed to the whole thing from the beginning. But your mother was afraid for you and your sister, with your father being in prison and all. Everybody thought there was going to be a war, you see. And there were rumors that the government planned to send children to work on Soviet farms, so she wanted to protect you. And when she found out there was a way of sending the two of you to America through the Catholic Church, your mother was one of the first ones to put your names on the list. And no one could stop her, I tell you. No one. —It's curious how the Church took you away and now it has brought you back.

LUCA: Do you want to go inside?

TIO LALO: I don't pray anymore. But if you want to.

LUCA: I do.

(Angelic music plays.)

Fresh Water from the River Ariguanabo

Sound of church bells announcing the morning. Luciana wears a dressing gown. She is listening to music from a Walkman. Hortensia enters with a basin of water and a white towel hanging from her shoulder.

HORTENSIA: I brought you some fresh mineral water from the springs . . .

LUCIANA: Oh, Señora Hortensia.

HORTENSIA: It's my duty. Fresh mineral water is good for the skin. I see you always carry your music with you.

LUCIANA: Everywhere I go.

HORTENSIA: Oh, I stopped listening to music on the radio.

LUCIANA: You don't like music?

HORTENSIA: Oh, yes . . . too much. That's why I don't listen to it. If I turn on the radio, I can't do anything else but sing and dance. And there's always something around here that needs my attention. The saints say that disorder brings confusion and misfortune. I wake up at five, I drink café looking at the last of the moon, then I start my day.

(Luciana takes off her dressing gown and cleans herself with the water.)

Are you single or married now?

LUCIANA: Divorced.

HORTENSIA: Ah, you're a modern woman.

LUCIANA: Oh no, Señora Hortensia, I'm not that modern.

HORTENSIA: Well, you're young and full of life . . . Here a woman like you not only has to be careful with men, but with spirits.

LUCIANA: Spirits.

HORTENSIA: Of course, there are spirits everywhere—in trees, rivers, wandering the streets.

There was one spirit who fell in love with me. He must've seen me naked coming out of the bathtub, because I felt his presence, like a cold wind. I had to cover myself with a towel. Oh, he followed me for weeks after that. I could feel him behind me like a shadow. He would leave messages everywhere. I'd find rose petals on my sink, or a cat would all of a sudden come into the kitchen with a ribbon in its mouth.

And I must say, I liked the attention too. It had been a while since anybody laid eyes on me. All of a sudden, I'd find myself powdering my face in the afternoons. I was

putting perfume behind my ears and on my bosom, until
I realized what I was doing. And I had to pray to get him
away and cleanse my whole being with an egg.

—Oh, the body never forgets love, Luciana. It has its
own time and memories. Sometimes I lie awake at night on
that old mattress my husband bought when we got married. I lie there in a hole where the mattress sinks from all
those years we made love, and I think to myself, Oh I knew
love . . . I knew love . . . And the old days come back, like a
forgotten season and restore all of what I was and am.
(Sighs) Oh, love . . .

LUCIANA: Yes, I know . . .

HORTENSIA: I know you do . . . I can see it on your face. I can see
a man sitting on top of your eyebrows. Am I right?

LUCIANA: You are.

HORTENSIA: And if you don't do something about it, he'll leave
footprints all over your features and make wrinkles . . . The
lines from sadness aren't good. The wrinkles from laughter yes, because they till and plow the face . . . *(Touches her
face)* But it's interesting, you don't have any lines. Let me
see the palm of your hand. *(Pause)* Your hand looks like the
hand of a young girl.

LUCIANA: How do you know there's a man?

(Basilio and Samuel enter holding a tray with coffee cups.)

BASILIO *(In a loud voice)*: Breakfast!

SAMUEL: Did you sleep well, Señora Luciana?

LUCIANA: Yes, as well as can be.

SAMUEL: Did the fireflies help with your dreams?

LUCIANA: I dreamt that I was walking by a river.

HORTENSIA: Ah, water . . . Good. The Ariguanabo river came to
greet you.

SAMUEL: Have you met with the pope many times, Señora Luciana?

BASILIO: Samuel, not many people get to talk to the pope, if anything they only get to kiss his ring.

SAMUEL: But you'll get to meet him now when you go back to the
city.

LUCIANA (*Going along, not wanting to ruin their enthusiasm*): Well,
that's what all the reporters are hoping for . . .

SAMUEL: Oh, I can just see Luciana sitting in a room with all
these men in skirts and all of them whispering about the
museum: one cups his ear, the other one whispers, from
bishop to bishop and cardinal to cardinal . . .

HORTENSIA (*Lifts her arms*): And after so many holy ears the
museum will be blessed! Right, Luciana?

LUCIANA (*With hesitation*): Well, actually . . . I've never . . . it will
be my first time . . . (*Fiercely determined to tell the truth*) —
Yes, it will be my first time.

SAMUEL: Even better. The pope is probably tired of the same
priests asking for money to paint their churches . . .

HORTENSIA: I think we stand a pretty good chance, don't you?

LUCIANA: Yes . . . yes . . . of course . . . Except sometimes I'm not
sure what exactly you want me to do . . .

SAMUEL: Mamá, you haven't told her. You can't expect her to do
anything! . . .

HORTENSIA: Please come, let us show you . . .

(*The brothers open a panel to reveal a wall full of drawers
holding religious objects, such as saints, brass crowns, brass
halos, reliquaries, rosaries, ribbons, wooden crutches, silver
hearts, silver hands, retablos, etc. It is a magical place that
looks like an altar. An angelic aria plays.*)

This is the Museum of Dreams . . .

LUCIANA: My God! . . .

BASILIO: These are just a few of all the miracles that came last
month. (*Hands Luciana a file*)

LUCIANA: May I see . . .

(The lights change, taking on an ethereal quality. The sound of a Tibetan bell. As Luciana opens the file and begins to read, each person who sent the miracle appears on the stage.)

FAUSTINO *(Wears an old straw hat)*: My name is Faustino Angel León. Carpenter and painter, residing at Compostela Street, Number 6A . . . On the 9th of September my father left the country and told me to take his little statue of the Virgin to the wilderness and place it in a river. When I got to the river, and placed the statue in the water, the statue turned into a goldfish, then it turned into a beautiful woman with long hair who disappeared swimming in the green river. She just vanished like sugar in water.

BASILIO: We have subfiles pertaining to the specific miracles the saints have performed. Files on love, work . . . Then there are cases like this one which we haven't labeled . . .

(Sound of the Tibetan bell.)

AMPARO *(Wears rollers in her hair)*: My name is Amparo de las Rosas. I am a seamstress residing at Cespedes Street. On the 7th of May the only thing my husband and I had to eat was a miserable potato that I fried in a pan with some rancid lard. That night my husband, Isidro, and I kneeled down in front of the altar and prayed for food. The next morning a flock of birds flew into the house, and I told Isidro to close all the windows to catch some of those God-sent creatures. The house and the patio were full of parrots, turkeys, doves, even birds I'd never seen.

That was our miracle because Isidro and I had food for a month. Later that day we heard on the news that an old tree had fallen on a bird cage at the zoo and hundreds of birds had escaped. But those birds that flew into our house weren't from the zoo. That was our miracle.

HORTENSIA: We want the church to acknowledge these miracles, Luciana, and we want you to help us. We want to make the museum a public building.

(The lights return to normal. Basilio closes the panel. Luciana walks to center stage.)

LUCIANA *(To the audience, lost in thought)*: I walk away from it all. I don't know what to do . . . I'm dumbstruck . . .

SAMUEL *(Following her, from a distance)*: Señora Luciana.

LUCIANA: I walk and walk . . . So many thoughts passing through my head, fast, like houses one sees from a train window . . . I don't know where I'm going . . .

SAMUEL: Señora Luciana, what did we do?

LUCIANA: I walk and walk . . . No, I can't go on pretending . . .

BASILIO *(Joining Samuel)*: What happened?

SAMUEL: Señora, what did we do!

BASILIO: Luciana . . .

(The brothers stand at a distance.)

LUCIANA: No, I have to walk . . . I have to . . . get away from it all . . .

HORTENSIA: Let her be . . . Let her be . . . Come inside . . .

BASILIO *(Approaching Luciana)*: Are you all right?

LUCIANA: Yes.

BASILIO: Come with me.

SAMUEL: Can I get you some water?

LUCIANA: No, I'm fine.
    I'd like to talk to you, Hortensia.

HORTENSIA: What is it, Luciana?

LUCIANA: I'm sorry. I've made a mistake . . . I should've explained before . . .

BASILIO: Explain what?

LUCIANA: Oh, I don't know if you would understand . . . it's all
    wrong . . .

SAMUEL: Wrong?

LUCIANA: Yes, me . . . I feel terrible . . . I'm not the right person . . .
    it's a mistake . . . I have to apologize to you.

SAMUEL: You haven't done anything wrong, Señora Luciana . . .
    Did you hear what she said, Mamá?

HORTENSIA: We're the ones who feel awful, Lucy . . . Our house,
    the lack of food . . .

BASILIO: Mamá was saying that if we knew last month that you
    were coming, we would've killed a pig and roasted it in your
    honor . . .

HORTENSIA: We just wish we had more to offer you . . . We feel
    bad that you've come from so far . . . Oh, if we were living
    in other times, I would've made new curtains and hung
    them inside the house. We would've painted a little. But
    nowadays there's no fabric or paint to be found.

*(Luciana takes a moment to look at this family. She's touched
by their purity and generosity.)*

LUCIANA: Hortensia . . . I don't know what I can do for the muse-
    um . . . But I'll try to do the best I can.

(Music plays. Lights on Luca and Delita. Luca carries a suitcase.)

LUCA: They told me to bring food, aspirin, soap, and I came pre-
    pared. Tell me what do you want to eat? *(He opens the suit-
    case. She's surprised to see all the food)* Beans, rice, soup, pis-
    tachios . . . What do you want? Vegetables, dry shrimps,
    pasta, nuts, cheese, Jell-O . . . What do you want? What do
    you want?

DELITA: I've never seen so much food.

LUCA: I told you I came prepared. Taste these biscuits. *(Gives her a biscuit. She takes a bite and smiles)* Good enh?!

DELITA: They taste like paradise.

LUCA: Rice, minestrone, black beans . . . What do you want me to make you?

DELITA: I haven't had a biscuit in so long. I can't think now. *(All of a sudden he notices tears in her eyes)*

LUCA: It's not supposed to make you cry.

DELITA *(Hides her tears)*: I'm crying from I don't know what. I've never seen so many things to eat. I feel like I'm being covered with a blanket of food.

LUCA: Don't cry. Let's go to your house. We have everything we need, and what we don't have we'll do without.

Reading Her Journal

SAMUEL *(Sits on the floor, browsing through Luciana's diary)*: "December 2nd: I'm preparing for the trip . . . January 4th: Luca sent email . . . He says he misses me . . . January 3rd: All of a sudden I've gone back to my childhood with Luca . . ."

(Hortensia enters with a broom.)

"January sixth: Just want the trip to end . . . December 31st: I'm preparing my luggage . . ."

HORTENSIA: Leave that alone—

SAMUEL: Wait. "January 3rd . . ."

HORTENSIA: Leave it alone . . .

SAMUEL: ". . . I'm in a quandary . . . January 7th: Wandered through the streets."

HORTENSIA: It's private . . . Put it down . . .

SAMUEL: So are miracles and we read them . . .

HORTENSIA: It's different.

SAMUEL: "January 10th: Spoke to a bishop about the—"

HORTENSIA: Leave it alone, I said. *(Slaps the book out of his hands)*

SAMUEL: But, Mamá, it says . . . it says that . . .

HORTENSIA: I don't care what it says . . . I don't care . . .

SAMUEL: She spoke to a bishop about the . . . museum . . . she writes that she . . .

HORTENSIA: What bishop?

SAMUEL: A bishop . . . That's what it said in the book . . .

HORTENSIA: Oh yeah . . .

SAMUEL: Yes . . .

HORTENSIA: Where is this bishop from?

SAMUEL: I don't know. You knocked the book out of my—

HORTENSIA: Well, pick it up and see . . .

SAMUEL: Now I forgot . . . *(Skims through the pages)* January 9th or 10th . . . Here it is: "Spoke to a bishop about the museum, Salvatore Caprile, from Casino . . ."

HORTENSIA: Sounds like an important man, with a name like that. Go on.

SAMUEL: "Plans to schedule a meeting with Hortensia and me . . ."

HORTENSIA: A meeting with me?

SAMUEL: That's what it says.

HORTENSIA: Put it away . . . put it away.

SAMUEL: Don't you want to know—?

HORTENSIA: Oh my! I have to do something!

SAMUEL: You're going to an important meeting, Mamá.

HORTENSIA: And so it says . . . *(Looks at her dress)* I'm going to have to look presentable, Samuel . . .

SAMUEL: Don't worry, Mamá. I'll polish your shoes . . .

(Hortensia starts to leave in a rush.)

Where are you going?

HORTENSIA: I'm going to borrow a dress from Zoila . . . I have to go . . . I have to go . . .

(Basilio enters.)

BASILIO: Where are you going in such a hurry?
HORTENSIA: I'm going to the city. I'm going to the city . . .

(Hortensia exits.)

BASILIO: What's going on with Mamá?
SAMUEL: She's meeting with a bishop . . .
BASILIO: A bishop?
SAMUEL: She's going to an important meeting with a bishop . . .
BASILIO: What are you doing with that book? Were you reading it?
SAMUEL *(Thrilled)*: She wrote about us . . .
BASILIO *(Takes the journal and reads)*: "Here, I can only anticipate the gifts that come with each day, whether it's a walk to the square with Basilio or a smile from Samuel."

(Basilio looks at Samuel and smiles.
The lights come up on Luciana.)

SAMUEL: What does she mean by that?
BASILIO: I don't know . . .

(The brothers continue reading the journal as they exit.
General Viamonte enters and approaches Luciana.)

LUCIANA: January 12th. An interrogation with General Viamonte
GENERAL VIAMONTE: Señora Luciana María, can I see your papers?
LUCIANA: Here's my passport.
GENERAL VIAMONTE: How long have you been in the country?
LUCIANA: More than twelve days . . .
GENERAL VIAMONTE: What's your involvement with the museum?
LUCIANA: I'm simply staying at Hortensia's. Is there a problem, compañero?

GENERAL VIAMONTE: The new laws don't allow tourists to stay in private homes.

LUCIANA: I'm not a tourist, compañero. I'm a journalist. I'm writing an article about the museum.

GENERAL VIAMONTE: Is that all you're doing?

LUCIANA: For the moment, yes. Unless there's another place that I should write about.

GENERAL VIAMONTE: Come with me, compañera . . .

LUCIANA: Where are you taking me?

GENERAL VIAMONTE: Come with me.

(The panel opens up. Lights come up on the altar. We hear an Afro-Cuban lullaby. Luca enters.)

LUCA *(Facing the audience)*: I went to the house we used to visit every summer . . . the place looked withered and old, as if the sea had entered the house. But the sign of the villa still read: VILLA BAHIA DE LA LUNA . . . The old swing was still there swaying in the breeze . . . and the hum of mother's song in the air, telling you to come back.

(The lights fade to black.)

ACT TWO

Luca and Luciana each stand in a square of light. As in Act One, each is in their own space, facing the audience. Behind them the rest of the characters stand in shadows.

Writing a Farewell Letter

LUCA: Dear Sister . . .

LUCIANA: Dear Brother . . .

LUCA: Dear Blue Parakeet, When shall I see you, how and where?

LUCIANA: You think I don't feel how much you want to see me!

LUCA: Dearest Sister, Dear Monkey Face, Can you sense that I'm writing about you?

LUCIANA: Can you sense that I'm writing about you?!

LUCA: Dearest Sister . . . My Summer Moth . . . Because once we were brother and sister . . .

LUCIANA: Because we are brother and sister!

LUCA: Because once we were mother and father to each other . . .

LUCIANA: Dear Brother, Dear Dark Bird of My Heart . . .

LUCA: Dear Sister . . .

LUCIANA: Because I can only love you best when you're far away, I've chosen to love you in the distance.

LUCA: Dear Sister, My Blue Parakeet, Because we've never spoken of the past . . .

LUCIANA: Because we've never spoken of the past! Because I looked for the meaning of our love in dictionaries, encyclopedias . . . Because it's wrong! It's wrong!

LUCA: Dear Sister, Dark Love, I've tried to subtract you from my being. But what's left if I subtract you from my blood? A half sky . . .

LUCIANA: Less summer . . .

LUCA: A half moon . . .

LUCIANA: Less June and July . . .

(Luciana walks out of her square of light.)

LUCA: My Dear Sister . . .

The Possibility That It's All a Dream

LUCIANA *(To audience)*: Why is it that I can't close my eyes, that I can't sleep? Or am I already sleeping? Am I dreaming all this? When I walk by the seawall in Havana, I see people sitting there waiting for the last of the light to end, like moths that gather around a light bulb. They search for whatever light the sea can illuminate. Whatever dimness is left before they enter the night without electricity. I just want to turn off the light in my mind, in that room I can't get to.

If Only It Could Be

Sound of the Tibetan bell. Hortensia is holding a green dress, a 1950s-style hat and a paper bag. She places the dress in front of her body and looks into an invisible mirror.

HORTENSIA: If I wear Zoila's dress, I'll have to wear a girdle. But it's too hot to wear a girdle. And if I wear this old hat I might look too elegant, sort of like Queen Elizabeth . . . But why not? I'm meeting an important bishop . . .

(Sound of the Tibetan bell. The lights come up on Samuel and Basilio standing in front of a telescope. Basilio is trying to focus the lenses.)

SAMUEL: Do you see anything yet?

BASILIO: I can see the moon.

SAMUEL: I know you can see the moon . . . but can you see inside her room?

BASILIO: I'm trying to see how the lenses work!

SAMUEL: This shit doesn't work. *(Walks away from the telescope)*

BASILIO: Of course it works. We just have to figure it out. This is for looking at things that are real far away, like the moon . . .

SAMUEL: Then, why don't we go up to the mountains and look from there?

BASILIO: Why don't we go up to the mountains, he says! Should we go to the moon, too! . . .

(Sound of the Tibetan bell. The lights come up on Luciana holding her journal by the light of the kerosene lamp.)

LUCIANA: If I tell Hortensia I was interrogated by the militia she might get upset. I mustn't tell her anything . . .

(Sound of the Tibetan bell. The lights come up on Luca and Tio Lalo.)

TIO LALO: Why hasn't your sister come by to visit me?

LUCA: She's working, Tio. She's dealing with the pope.

TIO LALO: And this pope never sleeps, never eats, never has any time off?

(Sound of the Tibetan bell. The lights come up on Delita tying a shoelace around a red piece of cloth.)

DELITA:

> A red candle,
> two dead lizards tied together with his shoelace,
> a red-and-black ribbon tied around
> seven needles dipped in my blood.
> This is how I'm going to make him love me.

(Sound of the Tibetan bell. The lights come up on Samuel and Basilio standing by the telescope.)

SAMUEL: And if we take off some of the lenses?

BASILIO: Then we'll see less, stupid . . .

SAMUEL: Isn't that what we want?

BASILIO: You know, you're a real knucklehead!

(Sound of the Tibetan bell. The lights come up on Luciana reading her article.)

LUCIANA: "Pope John Paul II is expected to arrive in two days. Workers have been hanging thousands of posters. Communist Party activists ripped down pictures of the pope in one Havana neighborhood."

(Lights up on Hortensia in front of the invisible mirror. She's trying on the dress to see how it fits.)

HORTENSIA: If only I had those earrings I traded for a pair of shoes . . . but then I wouldn't have Sunday shoes. I'll have to tell Samuel to paint two lines behind my legs, like the women did in the forties, so the bishop thinks I'm wearing stockings.

(Sound of the Tibetan bell. The lights come up on Luciana.)

LUCIANA: Little by little I realize why I'm playing this role, why I can't face myself . . . why I am living a lie . . .

(Sound of the Tibetan bell. The lights come up on Luca.)

LUCA: By the seawall I sit on one place and another . . . Perhaps in some terrible way I can be your brother like this in the distance.

(Sound of the Tibetan bell. The lights come up on Delita.)

DELITA:

    A hair from his chest
    and my eyelash
    wrapped in rose petals and cinnamon powder.
    I repeat his name three times . . .
    Luca, Luca, Luca . . .

(Sound of the Tibetan bell.)

HORTENSIA: Oh, Mamá Rita, if you could look down from the sky and see that it's finally happening. Just any day now, I'll be sitting with a bishop showing him all the miracles. I never thought I'd live to see the day. I know the bishop is going to be surprised when he sees the miracles. I'm even going to show him the one, about a woman who levitated . . . Imagine if that happened to me in the meeting . . . me, with my bag, in the middle of a meeting levitating . . . That would get the pope's attention . . . he'd make the museum a public building immediately . . . and I'd be famous like Matías Pérez, the balloonist who disappeared in the sky . . .

(Sound of the Tibetan bell. The lights come up on Samuel and Basilio and the telescope. Basilio is looking through the lenses. He moves away from the telescope.)

BASILIO: Forget it! Piece of shit.

SAMUEL: Who gave it to you?

BASILIO: Elisa the widow . . .

SAMUEL: When did you become her friend?

BASILIO: I saw her bathing in the river yesterday . . .

SAMUEL: I don't think I've seen her leave her house since her husband died . . .

BASILIO: Well, I have. She took off her clothes and swam naked . . . She was holding a paper boat full of flowers.

SAMUEL: What for?

BASILIO: Her husband who drowned out at sea.

SAMUEL: Some people say she's gone to hell with herself.

BASILIO *(Looks through the telescope again)*: She's just in pain. When she came out of the water, she slowly got dressed and walked to her house. I followed her. When she got to her house, she left her door open, so I could come inside.

SAMUEL: And you did?

BASILIO: Yes . . . Then, she left the room and came back with some clothes, and she signaled for me to wear them . . . They were her husband's clothes . . .

SAMUEL: You wore the dead man's clothes?

BASILIO: Sure. She wanted for me to be Juan Jose Silvestre . . . to make love to her as her husband . . .

SAMUEL: And you did?

BASILIO: I pretended she was Luciana María . . .

SAMUEL (*Looks in the direction of Luciana's room*): She'll leave soon, Basilio . . . She'll forget about us . . . and we'll be left alone in this miserable town, without a train station. Then everything will be the same. The house. The streets.

BASILIO: I feel strange, Samuel . . .

SAMUEL: I'm sure, after having sex like a dead man.

BASILIO: No. Sad. I don't think you and I have really known what it's like to have someone . . .

SAMUEL: You mean love?

(Samuel looks in the direction of Luciana's room. She has turned off the light from the kerosene lamp, and sits on the floor by the light of a candle.)

BASILIO: Yes. Those two, Juan Jose Silvestre and the widow must've loved each other. She started crying when we were doing it. I couldn't make her stop . . . at one point I felt like she wasn't there, as if she had gone somewhere else to meet him . . . She asked me to hit her, and I didn't want to but I did . . . then I got afraid . . . I thought something bad had happened to her . . . that I had—

SAMUEL: Killed her?

BASILIO: Yes.

SAMUEL: Is that what it's all about, to love until you feel that you're dying?

BASILIO: Maybe.

The Future of the Museum

LUCIANA: January 15th: Midday. A meeting with General Viamonte.

(General Viamonte enters. Luciana covers herself with a shawl. A desk and two chairs are brought on. Luciana and Hortensia sit to the left of the desk. General Viamonte walks around as he interrogates Luciana and Hortensia.)

GENERAL VIAMONTE: When I heard from my daughter, Melva, that you were going to help with the museum, I thought to myself we seem to have an important foreigner in our town.

HORTENSIA: She's not a foreigner, Viamonte . . . she was born here.

GENERAL VIAMONTE: She's a foreigner to me! When did you leave the country, señora?

LUCIANA: 1961.

GENERAL VIAMONTE: Ah! The Pedro Pan flights. The 14,000 children that were shipped away to the States . . .

HORTENSIA: Compañero Viamonte . . .

GENERAL VIAMONTE: Don't interrupt me, compañera. I'm talking to Luciana María. So, the Pedro Pan project, they called it, like the children's book about the boy who runs away to never-never land and never grows up . . . That's a young age to have a child fly alone on an airplane . . .

LUCIANA: I wasn't alone. I was with my brother.

GENERAL VIAMONTE: Even worse—two children.

LUCIANA: I thought we were going to talk about the museum!

GENERAL VIAMONTE: We are—it's very Christian of Hortensia to think that you could do something for this museum . . . it shows that we haven't managed to abolish the colonial mentality of having foreigners taking care of our problems—

LUCIANA: I think you're mistaken. I took it upon myself—

GENERAL VIAMONTE: No I'm not mistaken. When Hortensia came to us with the idea of this museum, it appealed to us.

Anybody would want to finance a Museum of Dreams . . .
But then—

HORTENSIA: You funded the Museum of Humor that was opened
down the road! I'm sure it took plenty of money to build it.

GENERAL VIAMONTE: We need to laugh, compañera. We need to
laugh at how we live despite all the difficulties imposed on
us . . . It's what keeps us going, our humor.

HORTENSIA: Our faith, compañero . . . faith. Go to the river . . . go
to the seawall in Havana and you'll see how many oblations
have been offered to the Virgin of Regla . . . there's the
Procession of Miracles every year.

GENERAL VIAMONTE: That's once a year, compañera . . . and it
involves a few locals celebrating an old tradition . . .

HORTENSIA: Tradition! It has to do with people who pray who
have dreams.

GENERAL VIAMONTE: But it has nothing to do with tourists coming from afar. —It's certainly not about exposing things
which tend to be overdrawn, like those silly miracles that
have been documented in books.

HORTENSIA: You know well my miracles are simple acts—

GENERAL VIAMONTE: All miracles have an element of exaggeration! In every religion: Buddha making five hundred ele-
phants grow out of a lotus flower, Mohammed cutting the
moon in two pieces . . .

LUCIANA: For a man who doesn't believe in miracles, you know
more about them than I do.

GENERAL VIAMONTE: I read about things I dislike, compañera, so
I can understand why I feel resistance and aversion. (Pause)
We live in an age of reason, of natural science. We take pride
in the real. Our system gave me a pair of shoes, a home, a
refrigerator. If Compañera Hortensia wants to call our
accomplishments miracles, then these are the miracles
that need to be exhibited in her museum . . .

LUCIANA: Those are not miracles.

GENERAL VIAMONTE: Then what are miracles?

HORTENSIA: It's a pity, compañero, but I don't think you will ever understand.

LUCIANA: It has to do with faith, compañero.

GENERAL VIAMONTE: Faith. Faith. And what do you know about faith? You come from a so-called religious land, dollar bills that read: "In God We Trust." What devil do they worship there? It can't be in the name of God that your country has tried to blockade and starve a small island like ours for years.

LUCIANA: I didn't come here to talk about politics.

GENERAL VIAMONTE: But you certainly have opinions! How did you get involved in all this religious hysteria? *(Picks up her passport)* Your visa is strictly for journalistic purposes. Why aren't you in Havana following the pope?

LUCIANA: Well, I got a letter from Hortensia.

HORTENSIA: My letters, compañero . . . she responded to one of my letters . . .

GENERAL VIAMONTE *(To Luciana)*: You're lying!

HORTENSIA: The letters we sent abroad when we found out the pope was coming.

GENERAL VIAMONTE: What letters? All the letters you tried to send never left this country.

HORTENSIA: What do you mean?

GENERAL VIAMONTE: We weren't going to have any commotion around here, compañera. Did you actually think we were going to have the pope in this town?

HORTENSIA *(Looks at Luciana in disbelief)*: What are you talking about, compañero?

GENERAL VIAMONTE: You live in a world of fantasy, with angels and spirits, and you don't want to face reality . . .

HORTENSIA: No. What happened to my letters! What happened to my letters!

GENERAL VIAMONTE: Don't get emotional.

HORTENSIA: What happened to my letters!

GENERAL VIAMONTE: Maybe one letter slipped by, but most of them are in our possession. We have a democratic process in this country, Luciana . . . A meeting was held in this town as to whether this museum should be made into a public building and most people voted against it.

HORTENSIA: Lies . . . lies . . . that's a bunch of lies . . .

GENERAL VIAMONTE: She knows well that we're not interested in tourist attractions.

LUCIANA: But her museum—

GENERAL VIAMONTE: Nobody wants tourists in this town. You can see what's happening in Havana—prostitution, corruption. That's why we voted against it.

HORTENSIA: It's a bunch of lies. You passed around a few papers. Who knows how many were signed! Who knows how many were kept away—like my letters . . .

GENERAL VIAMONTE: You see? Hysteria. That's all . . . religious hysteria . . . *(Lights a cigar)*

HORTENSIA *(Gathers her strength and rage)*: All these years you've tried to sink me down, to bury me alive. A few days from now all the ceremonies of the pope will end. Luciana will leave and the two of us will have to live long after all of this is over, in this small town, on this little island. But let me tell you something, compañero, for thirty years I've wanted to spit in your face. Thirty years building up the courage . . . this froth, and bitter spit in my mouth . . . But now that I face you, I believe my spit is too clean for your face. If ever I curse anybody in my lifetime then let it be you, Agusto Viamonte. *(Trying to show his indifference, he smokes his cigar)* May those cigars you smoke burn a hole on your tongue and in your lungs, and may those holes fester. Death I don't wish you. I leave that to God. May you continue to breathe the same simple beautiful air I breathe in this town. Good day, compañero!

(*Luciana and Hortensia exit. General Viamonte follows.*

The sound of Luciana's voice reciting articles she has written about the pope becomes a cacophony of journalistic writing mixed with Gregorian chants.

The panel opens to reveal the museum's miracles. Luciana enters. She starts looking through the miracles. Sound of the Tibetan bell.)

Another Miracle

GUSTAVO: Gustavo Soto is my name. I am a clerk at the post office on Center Street. At approximately 6:30 in the morning I dreamt that there was an eclipse and my ears had grown down to the floor . . . and I didn't know why this was happening to me . . . The only thing I could think in my dream was that God was going to speak to me and I needed enough room in my being to house his voice . . . and sure enough a sacred voice whispered something to me and I was told to wake up and run out of the house, which I did. My house was up in flames from the pot of milk my wife had forgotten on the burner . . . I tell people that was no ordinary dream, that was Santa Candelaria who leaned over me and whispered my salvation.

The Museum and Luciana

HORTENSIA: Reading the miracles?

LUCIANA: Yes. Each one is like a little story.

Are you prepared to go to the city today and meet with the bishop?

HORTENSIA: No, I've decided not to go.

LUCIANA: Are you going to let that miserable bastard Viamonte dictate what to do with the museum?

HORTENSIA: I'm not closing the museum.

LUCIANA: Then do something!

HORTENSIA: The spirits came to me last night and told me that it wasn't the right time . . .

LUCIANA: And do you believe that is the right thing to do?

HORTENSIA: Yes.

LUCIANA: Hortensia, why don't—

HORTENSIA: I'm not giving up, Luciana.

LUCIANA: Then fight. You're strong. I'm sure you can appeal your case in court. Don't let him stop you.

HORTENSIA: Waiting is a form of fighting.

LUCIANA *(With contained anger)*: It seems like this whole island is always waiting! Waiting! Waiting for something to happen. And nothing ever happens. Who's going to be the first one to stop waiting! Who's going to be the first!

HORTENSIA: You have your ways . . . You come from a different world.

LUCIANA: No, I come from the same world.

HORTENSIA: The pope coming here means nothing. It's all about bringing money to the island.

LUCIANA: You don't know that.

HORTENSIA: I do. I live here. Nothing will change. *(Points to the patio)* You saw those three white pigeons in the patio this morning when you were hanging your clothes—they were three ladies with large purses who visited my dreams. Messengers who came to me last night.

LUCIANA *(Losing her patience)*: Oh, Hortensia, I'm sorry, I can't live my life that way! Just give up the museum! Give up on the whole thing! Go ahead and put it in his hands . . .

(The panel opens. The altar rumbles. A few of the relics fall to the floor.)

HORTENSIA: That is Elegua, the trickster—the opener of the ways—making noise . . . He will tell me when to move forward with the museum. Mamá Rita always said, "You must learn to endure what you can't change."

(*Luciana realizes that Hortensia and the museum possess higher powers.*)

LUCIANA: You know, Hortensia, all of this sort of fell in my lap— you, the museum, Basilio and Samuel—I never got any letters from you. One day I just stumbled into this place. Samuel said, "Are you here to see my mother?" And those words must've rung true . . . It was by coincidence . . . (*Catches herself*) —No, like you say, there's no coincidence.

HORTENSIA: Why did you choose to stay with us?

LUCIANA: Because for the moment I needed a sense of place, to belong. And wouldn't you like to live in a place called the Museum of Dreams?

HORTENSIA: I live here. I'm asking you.

LUCIANA: I need to believe that miracles exist. I've been running away from myself . . .

HORTENSIA: You don't have to tell me . . . I saw it on your face the first time we spoke.

LUCIANA: I need to believe there is a miracle for me.

HORTENSIA: Miracles are the obedience of dreams . . . they take their time making their way to the world. They have their own system of making their way to us.

Love is a grave matter, Luciana. Just remember that, from the beginning, everything in life is trying to find its place but also its absence. And already from the beginning the absence had begun . . . Go find your brother. Find him.

LUCIANA: How do you know . . . ?

HORTENSIA: Find him. And when you see him, send me a note like this one, and I'll hang it in the museum.

(*Hortensia exits.*)

The Danzón of Unbearable Urges

Luciana alone. A danzón plays. Basilio and Samuel enter dancing.
Basilio takes Luciana to dance.

BASILIO: Come on Luciana . . .

LUCIANA: I don't know how to dance.

BASILIO *(Dancing with her)*: A Cuban who doesn't know how to
　　dance. This is how Mami and Papi used to dance. Was it
　　like this, Samuel?

SAMUEL *(Takes Luciana away from him)*: No, like this . . . like this . . .

BASILIO: That's not the way you dance danzón. You're moving
　　your hips too much . . . it's more on the feet. Like this . . .
　　(Demonstrates on his own)

LUCIANA *(Breaks away)*: You two dance . . . I'll watch.

(She brings them together to dance. The two brothers dance.)

BASILIO: You're moving your hips too much . . .

SAMUEL: And you're moving your arm as if we learned to dance
　　in the fields . . .

BASILIO: That's it! Slide your feet . . . if you mark the step and
　　slide your feet . . .

SAMUEL: You dance with him, Luciana . . .

(Suddenly the electricity goes out.)

BASILIO: Ah, fuckin' electricity . . .

SAMUEL: Just as we were getting the steps . . .

BASILIO: Every night the same thing . . . the electricity. We have
　　to go to bed early like birds . . .

SAMUEL: Now what do we do?

LUCIANA: We go to sleep, each one to his own room. Tomorrow
　　will be another day.

BASILIO *(To Luciana)*: Stay up a while longer . . . I want to know more about you.

(Pause.)

LUCIANA: Let's go for a walk.

Entering the Night without Electricity

LUCA: What do you do when the power gets cut off?

DELITA *(Holding a candle)*: I come here to the seawall and sit under the moon or I sit by a candle and bite my nails.

It's a sad silence, like a crime took place somewhere. Can you hear it now?

(The dialogue takes place in different spaces, but the conversations converge:)

LUCIANA: It's a dark night, as if somebody stole the light from the world.

SAMUEL: How old were you when you left the island?

LUCIANA: Eleven.

DELITA: You must not remember much about this place.

BASILIO: You're almost American . . .

LUCA: Are you saying that I'm American?

BASILIO: You were so young when you left.

LUCIANA: But I don't feel American.

DELITA: I always wanted to go.

SAMUEL: You know, big cities frighten me.

DELITA: There's so much I want to do.

SAMUEL: So much happening . . .

DELITA: So many places I'd like to go.

SAMUEL: I get something in my throat.

LUCA: And why don't you leave?

DELITA: Easy for you to say.

LUCA: Do you want a cigarette?

DELITA: Yes.

BASILIO: Our father always said, "If you have a nice shirt, you should have a tie. If you have a tie, you should have a jacket. If you have a jacket, you should have a hat. And if you have a hat, that means you could go somewhere." And those are things we don't have.

LUCIANA: All you need is to just want to go.

BASILIO: You must not remember much about this place.

LUCIANA *(Goes somewhere else in her mind)*: I do. My brother and I at the airport . . . my mother combing my hair . . .

DELITA: Who took care of you over there?

LUCA: At the beginning we were placed in a foster home.

LUCIANA: Hundreds of children . . .

LUCA: Every day this fury that our mother had abandoned us.

LUCIANA: Our mother was supposed to meet up with us.

LUCA: Everything seemed like a lie.

LUCIANA: Weeks passed. Months.

LUCA: All the flights stopped.

LUCIANA: The Missile Crisis.

LUCA: Our mother couldn't leave, and we couldn't come back.

DELITA: I never thought that life would be difficult up there.

LUCA: It was. I remember it as if it was yesterday. A cold town in Ohio. An old building falling apart . . . children and more children. The stench of urine.

LUCIANA: In Ohio I learned to speak English. In Ohio I discovered snow and winter. In Ohio my heart was circumcised.

LUCA: The only thing I liked about that place was a yellow bus taking us to school. The bus driver selling perfume . . .

LUCIANA: I remember buying a little bottle of perfume, putting it on my skin . . .

LUCA: They smell so pure those perfumes, so clean . . .

LUCIANA: I remember my brother smelling me, telling me I had stopped smelling like his sister.

LUCA: I used to jump the fence that separates the boys from the girls to see her.

LUCIANA: I used to spray a cloud of fragrance all around us, to erase every trace of who we were—

LUCA: Until one night we sense the smell of our skin.

LUCIANA: Then it happened, they separated us.

LUCA: They put me in a dump with drug addicts and drunks.

LUCIANA: From then on, all the girls at the home called me a whore . . . they'd pull up my dress and point to my parts. They'd say, "That's where he was, the brother."

LUCA: If only we could've stopped the world! Destruction, a war.

LUCIANA: The only way back to my brother was to close my eyes.

(*Luciana walks toward her brother.*)

LUCA: Eyes closed I began to float . . .

LUCIANA: Eyes closed I began to meet him in my mind . . .

LUCA: She'd become a playground as large as Africa . . .

LUCIANA: Day after day I'd meet him . . .

LUCA: I'd see her on every window . . .

LUCIANA: when I'm twelve, thirteen, fourteen . . .

LUCA: when I'm twelve, thirteen . . . one day I'm twenty.

LUCIANA: One day I'm nineteen.

LUCA: I call her up.

LUCIANA: He tells me he's bringing our mother with him.

LUCA: When I see my sister, I still see the little girl with the suitcase.

LUCIANA: He brings me Mamá as a present, like a doll from my childhood.

LUCA: Mamá makes us stand in front of her.

LUCIANA: She cooks.

LUCA: She can't stop cooking for us.

LUCIANA: With each meal she wants to fill the hunger, the absence.

LUCA: We eat and swallow the ten years of distance . . .

LUCIANA: Mamá wants us to become her children again . . .

LUCA: She sings. She wants to put things in order . . .

LUCIANA: I know what she means by order . . . I know . . . *(The pain rises. Her eyes are full of tears)* Oh God, one day I cry, I don't think I even know that I'm crying . . . *(She's lost in the memory)* I talk and talk and I don't even know that I'm talking. *(She shouts. She can't keep from shouting)* It's wrong! It's wrong! I tell Mamá to marry me off . . . to marry me off to the first man I find . . . I tell her this like a criminal who decides to turn himself in. I do it for her . . . I do it for him, because I can't do it for myself.

DELITA: It's starting to rain.

BASILIO: The rain has started to come down.

(Luciana looks up at the rain. She lets her face be bathed.)

DELITA: Let's go back inside.

(Luciana's mind returns to Samuel and Basilio.)

LUCA: No. Let's sit here and watch it come down.

(Delita stays looking at the gentle rain. Her eyes fill with tears. She looks at Luca, who is still immersed in the past. She turns back to the rain for comfort, and as a way of expressing her dismay.)

BASILIO: You love your brother.

LUCIANA: He was my mother, my father, my brother and sister, and also nothing. Nothing. So he could be everything. Everything.
    (She starts to trace all the places she mentions on Basilio's face) On his mouth the seaside. On his eyebrows my old school.

(Basilio embraces her. He kisses her. They exit. Samuel remains behind, alone and sad. The lights fade on him.)

DELITA: I want to go.

LUCA: Why?

DELITA: Because I have bad luck. I always seem to attract men who are sad or lost.

LUCA: Do you think I'm lost?

DELITA: No. Forget it. It's moments like this I wish I could take my eyes and put them in my purse. *(Swings her purse and makes circles in the air)*

LUCA: Look at me.

DELITA *(Gently)*: I don't think we should see each other anymore.

LUCA: Why?

DELITA: Because.

LUCA: Am I that awful?

DELITA: No. It's me. I was forewarned about this a thousand times.

LUCA: What?

DELITA: About meeting foreigners by the seawall.

LUCA: And why do you do it?

DELITA: Because for the moment one gets to live a little through them.

LUCA *(Touches her face tenderly)*: Delita.

DELITA: I'm not good at the touch and go. *(Tries to make light of the situation)* My friend Chuchi told me I have a weak heart and lungs, and the secret to all this is to hold your breath, like this. *(Holds her breath)*

LUCA *(Playfully)*: Stop that.

DELITA: No. Go. Leave. You don't want to see me cry.

LUCA: I'm not leaving until you look at me.

DELITA: Is she beautiful, your sister?

LUCA: She is to me.

DELITA: I thought she would be. I feel like I've already met her through you.

LUCA: You know, I never like to talk about her.

DELITA: Why?

LUCA: Because this always happens!

DELITA: I'm sorry. It's just that this is the first time I've ever met
somebody with your story.

LUCA: Let's go to your house.

DELITA: No. Let's stop this.

LUCA: I just wanted to lie next to you.

DELITA: Sooner or later, you'll go. It's better if I don't see you
anymore.

LUCA: Delita . . . Delita . . .

(Delita exits.)

Mercedita's Miracle

*The lights change, taking on an ethereal quality. Sound of the
Tibetan bell. Mercedita wears glasses and holds a white sheet.*

MERCEDITA: My name is Mercedita Perez. On the 1st of September, I was hanging some laundry to dry, and the face of
San Cristobal appeared before me on this sheet. I had sent
my children abroad, because my husband had been shot
fighting the rebels, and I wanted them to be safe. San
Cristobal came to tell me that my children were safe in a
small town up North.

(Sound of the Tibetan bell.)

Farewell to the Museum of Dreams

Music plays.

LUCIANA: January 20th: I write this as though I am claiming and
taking back with me a box of embraces . . . a box of dreams

... All that came my way on this trip ... the miracles ... the eyes of two men ... a jar of fireflies ... a jar of memories ...

Little Memories

All the characters stand behind Luciana. Sound of the Tibetan bell. Reprise. Memories, moments from the journey return as simple dialogue from the text:

SAMUEL *(Holds the jar full of fireflies)*: I was going to leave you this present in the room. In the old days people used to say that fireflies light the road to dreams.

(Sound of the Tibetan bell.)

BASILIO *(Brings the suitcase)*: Our father always said, "If you have a shirt, you should have a tie. If you have a tie, you should have a jacket ..."

(Sound of the Tibetan bell.)

GENERAL VIAMONTE: This so-called Museum of Dreams, has no future in this town. All miracles have an element of exaggeration ...

(Sound of the Tibetan bell.)

HORTENSIA: Sometimes I'm asleep and old spirits wake me up ... they come with invisible suitcases full of maps, pendulums ... they tell me how I should continue to build the museum ...

(Sound of the Tibetan bell.)

LUCA: I always thought that one day we would visit the island together, our old house, and that we would knock on the door and tell them we want to have a look.

(Luciana speaks to the audience, holding her suitcase. The rest of the characters slowly walk backward away from her.)

LUCIANA: I only had to close my eyes and take everything with me. Now it was time to find my way back to what I had left behind.

(Sound of the Tibetan bell.)

Houses without Electricity

Hortensia, Basilio and Samuel enter the stage with kerosene lamps, papers and the files containing the miracles. Samuel and Basilio sit on the floor.

HORTENSIA: Our house seems strange without Luciana.

SAMUEL: Yes, as if a wave from the sea came and took something away . . .

BASILIO: It seemed like she had always lived with us.

HORTENSIA: —Here, you file this stack.

BASILIO: We got more miracles this month than last month.

HORTENSIA: Probably because of the pope's visit.

BASILIO: It's better that the pope never got to see the museum.

HORTENSIA: Why?

BASILIO: Keeps us looking forward to something.

SAMUEL: What?

BASILIO: Working.

HORTENSIA *(Pulls out a file)*: I think all these miracles have to do with love.

BASILIO: I'll take them.

HORTENSIA: These have to do with illness.

SAMUEL: I'll take them.

HORTENSIA: I'm going to go rest. It's late. Good night.

SAMUEL: Good night.

BASILIO: Good night.

(Sound of the Tibetan bell.)

Life with You

LUCIANA: Tio Lalo . . . Tio Lalo . . .

TIO LALO *(Entering)*: Who's that?

LUCIANA: The door was open.

TIO LALO: Is that you, Luciana?

LUCIANA: Yes.

TIO LALO *(Hugs her)*: I thought I was never going to see you. Let me look at you. You have your mother's face. Where were you?

LUCIANA: I was in a town called Santiago de las Vegas.

TIO LALO: What for? Nobody lives there.

LUCIANA *(Laughs)*: Is my brother here?

TIO LALO *(Loudly)*: Luca! *(Pause)* He must be out in the patio. *(Loudly)* Luca!

(Sound of the Tibetan bell. Lights up on Samuel and Basilio.)

BASILIO: What do you think this miracle is about?

SAMUEL: A gleaming chair.

BASILIO: We can't call a file a gleaming chair.

SAMUEL: Reckoning then.

BASILIO: No.

SAMUEL: Affliction.

BASILIO: Affliction?

SAMUEL: Latitudes of pursuit.
BASILIO: What the hell is that?

(Sound of the Tibetan bell. Lights up on Luca)

LUCA: Luciana.
LUCIANA: Hello, Luca.

(An awkward pause.)

TIO LALO: Aren't you going to give your sister a hug? Or people
don't give hugs in the States.
LUCA: Of course.

(He hugs her. It is a cold embrace. There is a pause.)

TIO LALO: You just arrived in time for lunch. I was about to start
serving it.

(Tio Lalo exits.)

SAMUEL: Put it in this file. I just learned this new word.
BASILIO: What is it?
SAMUEL: Estuary.
BASILIO: What does that mean?
SAMUEL: The arm of the sea.
BASILIO: Oh God! You better stop reading poetry books.

*(Sound of the Tibetan bell. Luciana moves away, as if the
moment has become too much for her. She looks at the walls of
the house.)*

LUCIANA: The house seems smaller. In my mind it had higher
ceilings and I always thought there was another room.

LUCA: That's because you dreamed about it for so long. You didn't want to come back . . .

LUCIANA: No. Not after all these years . . .

(Luca knows that the house is their old nest and she can't go back there yet. He tries to be gentle with her. He knows it's bet- ter to look at the place through the eyes of the two children they were when they left.)

LUCA: —Remember the lizard cemetery we made, and all the hearts we carved on the tree trunk? The hearts are still there.

LUCIANA: Some marks never go away.

LUCA: No, they don't.

LUCIANA *(Trying to avoid where the conversation is heading)*: It's good that Tio Lalo stayed living here.

LUCA: Yes. But you seem tired.

LUCIANA: I am. I feel like I've aged ten years.

LUCA: No. You still look like a girl, like water that never ages.

LUCIANA: It's a malady, Luca. It's all a malady.

LUCA: No, it isn't. Look at me.

LUCIANA: My husband used to say I was sick, that I had gotten stuck in the past.

LUCA: Oh, he always thought we were fools. The whole family.

LUCIANA: No. There were some things that I kept. Childhood pic- tures of us. The old clothes. The red suitcase. He'd catch me opening it, and spreading the little clothes on the floor.

LUCA: And what did he want you to do, throw them away?

LUCIANA: He'd say he didn't understand it.

LUCA: Forget him. Come on, jump on my back and let me take you for a horsey ride . . .

LUCIANA: And what would Tio Lalo say?

LUCA: That we were the children who used to live here.

(Luciana jumps on Luca's back. He gives her a ride. They laugh. They are like children again. Then it happens—he stops and

she embraces him. She kisses him on his forehead, remaining there on his back like a little girl. There is silence. Time has stopped. The laughter turns into tears.)

Do you regret our past?

LUCIANA: I regret nothing. But you and I . . . we have to find a way . . .

LUCA: I'm learning how to be your brother again.

LUCIANA: You never stopped being that.

LUCA: For a long time I had thought about this moment, when we would finally talk . . .

LUCIANA: Me, too. I thought I had to find a way to tell it to myself, like a children's story that explains the world.

LUCA: And how would the story go?

LUCIANA: Two children dressed up in airport dreams. Two children who thought the world was going to end. Two children who only had each other.

(Sound of the Tibetan bell. Darkness, except for a shaft of light on Samuel and Basilio. Sound of the Tibetan bell.)

SAMUEL: Do you think when Luciana made love to you, she thought of her brother?

BASILIO: Yes, in my arms . . .

SAMUEL: In some ways we almost made love to each other through Luciana . . .

BASILIO: Maybe . . .

SAMUEL: You were full of light when she was here . . .

BASILIO: I felt like I had gone to the sky and back . . .

SAMUEL: Yes. Everything changed, didn't it? It seemed like we were seeing this whole place with new eyes. It was almost like a miracle, wasn't it?

BASILIO: Yes.

SAMUEL: You think we can file it as one?

BASILIO: I don't know if I can find the words.

SAMUEL: This morning I was thinking that if you love a person you must wish them well in life, even if you are sinking in a hole.

BASILIO: You sound like Mamá.

SAMUEL: No. I think I learned this from Luciana.

(Sound of the Tibetan bell.)

LUCIANA: Dear Hortensia, I'm sending you my miracle. My name is Luciana María.

LUCA: My name is Luca Manuel.

LUCIANA: I am a journalist living at 39 Forest Street, Providence, Rhode Island.

LUCA: I am a salesman living at 257 West 57th Street, New York.

LUCIANA: In the month of September 1961.

LUCA: In the month of September 1961. My sister and I used to dress up in airport dreams.

LUCIANA: We'd spend endless afternoons looking for airplanes in the sky.

(The music swells. The lights fade to black.)

END OF PLAY

A
BICYCLE
COUNTRY

PRODUCTION HISTORY

A Bicycle Country was commissioned by The Public Theater in New York City. *A Bicycle Country* premiered on December 10, 1999, at Florida Stage (Louis Tyrrell, Producing Director; Nancy Barnett, Managing Director) in Manalapan, Florida. It was directed by Benny Sato Ambush; the set design was by Kent Goetz, the costume design was by Lynda Peto, the lighting design was by Jim Fulton; the production stage manager was Suzanne Clement Jones. The cast was as follows:

JULIO	Gilbert Cruz
INES	Sol Miranda
PEPE	Oscar Riba

CHARACTERS

JULIO, a man in his forties

INES, a woman in her thirties

PEPE, a man in his thirties

TIME AND PLACE

Before the U.S. intervention on Cuban rafters in 1994.

SET

The set is a square wooden platform with a column in the middle. This platform becomes a raft in the second half, "Agua." To the right of the platform's column there are two wooden chairs, a table and an old trunk. Objects needed throughout the play are taken out of the trunk or brought onstage by the characters. A white screen (or cloth) on the upstage area frames the stage. A large round orange spotlight is reflected on the white screen for the day scenes and a large round white light is used for the night scenes. The white screen is used to project subtitles and can also change in color according to the mood of the scenes. For the last scene of the play the white screen should be raised to reveal a green landscape (if a cloth is used, it should drop).

TIERRA

Scene 1

"Tierra" is projected on the screen. A bolero plays. Julio is standing, strapped by a rope to a wooden board. The board leans against the column. Ines stands close to him. She writes a few of Julio's instructions on a small piece of paper. Pepe sits at the table, near Julio's wheelchair.

JULIO: I don't have an alarm clock. My eyes open at seven o'clock. That's the time I wake up. The first thing you give me are the pills. They are right here by the night table—

PEPE: He takes one of the pink ones, two of the yellow. Right, Julio? After he takes the pills you give him—

JULIO: After I take the pills, she gives me the bedpan.

PEPE: Yes . . . it's under the bed.

JULIO: I take two to five minutes on it. Sometimes more.

PEPE (*To Ines, trying to ease the situation*): That's a good time for you to occupy yourself doing something else. You can smoke a cigarette—

JULIO: No. She goes to the kitchen to heat up the water for my bath.

PEPE: Yeah, you go to the kitchen—

JULIO: At 7:10 I should be ready. She takes the bedpan and cleans me. When she finishes cleaning me, she gets rid of what's inside the pan. Then she goes to the kitchen to get the bucket of water for my bath, and she comes back to me—that's around 7:14 . . .

PEPE: 7:nothing, Julio! . . . (*Back to Ines*) I'll instruct you as you go along. Don't worry. I'll teach you.

JULIO: I want to be dressed by 7:30, and that is our goal.

PEPE: Yeah, no shoes till he's ready to stand.

JULIO (*Looks down at his feet*): I have to get used to the standing position. It's good for my circulation. We do this twice a day, when I get up in the morning and an hour before I go to sleep. —What time is it now?

INES: It's almost nine. At what time do you go to sleep?

JULIO: Sometimes nine . . . Sometimes eleven. It depends . . .

INES: What do I have to do to help you?

JULIO: Well, there are things that have to be done before I go to sleep. It's part of the nightly routine. Please, unstrap me. I'm ready to go to bed.

(*Ines unstraps Julio. She places her right shoulder under his arm to help him sit in the wheelchair.*)

I'll sit here for a bit to catch my breath. You can go to the kitchen and heat up some milk. I drink a glass of warm milk before I go to bed.

INES: You won't fall?

JULIO: I can hold myself up.

INES *(To Pepe)*: Would you help me in the kitchen? Show me
   where everything is kept.

PEPE: Sure.

(Ines and Pepe move off toward the kitchen.)

INES: Pepe, I want to talk to you.

PEPE: What's the matter?

INES: You didn't tell me . . . You didn't tell me everything had to be
   so . . . I don't know . . . so, paranh-pin-punh . . . so by the clock.

(Julio wheels himself close to them to hear the conversation.)

PEPE: I told you he likes things done a certain way . . .

INES: He's like a commander. I don't know if I can work under
   these conditions. I don't know if I can. I worked in a hospital, but I don't know if . . .

PEPE: He's a good man. You have to get—

JULIO *(In a loud voice)*: Pepe . . .

PEPE: He's calling me. *(In a loud voice)* Coming . . . *(Walks to Julio)*

JULIO: Is she all right?

PEPE: Yes . . . I mean . . . No. I think you're scaring her away.

JULIO *(In a loud voice)*: Ines.

INES *(Joining them)*: Yes.

JULIO *(To Pepe)*: Why don't you explain to her that it takes time
   getting me dressed?

PEPE *(Back to Ines)*: I've helped him—

JULIO: Why don't you explain to her, that if she follows my
   instructions we can make more use of time?

PEPE: He says—

INES: I heard.

JULIO: Explain to her that if she follows my method—

PEPE: You see, it takes time getting him up from—

INES: I understand.

PEPE: It's different when you can't do things on your own.

INES: How much is he going to pay me?

PEPE: Julio.

JULIO: Half of what I'll receive every month.

PEPE: He's going to get money for being on relief . . . He hasn't gotten it yet.

INES: So, how does he expect me to start working, when he doesn't have any money?

PEPE: Julio.

JULIO: Pepe, come here. Come close.

(Julio whispers something in Pepe's ear. Pepe nods. Julio unclasps a gold chain from around his neck. Pepe takes the chain and gives it to Ines.)

INES: What's this for?

JULIO: Your first salary. That's your pay.

INES: I'm not taking his chain.

JULIO: Why not? You can sell it or trade it for something.

PEPE: You see, he's paying you already. You can start working.

INES: No, give it back to him. He can pay me when he gets his money. Tell me what else needs to be done.

PEPE: He listens to the radio before he goes to sleep. And you have to give him one of the yellow pills.

INES: You'll have to excuse me, I want to change my shoes. These shoes bother me.

JULIO: You should make yourself at home. You can take off your shoes if you like.

INES: No, thank you. I don't like to walk barefoot.

(The lights change.)

Scene 2

"A Month Later" is projected on the screen. Julio is sitting in his wheelchair exercising. He lifts his arms up and down. Ines helps him with his right arm.

JULIO: That was twenty.

INES: Again.

JULIO: That was twenty-one.

INES: Again!

JULIO: Twenty-two.

INES: More!

JULIO: Twenty-three.

INES: Two more.

JULIO: I can't.

INES: You want to get better!

JULIO: I can't anymore!

INES: One more time.

JULIO: Twenty-four.

INES: Come on . . . You're strong.

JULIO: That's twenty-five . . .

INES: One more. Try again.

JULIO: That's it! No more!

INES: You can't rest now.

JULIO: You're killing me!

INES: You'll go to waste if you don't exercise.

JULIO: I can't do all the repetitions.

INES: To say "I can't" is to say "I won't" do it.

JULIO: It's too much.

INES: You want me to blow some air on your face? Are you fatigued?

JULIO: We're done for today.

INES: No. You have to do more.

JULIO: You're out of your mind. What do you think I am, an athlete?! I'm sick!

INES: You're better than you think you are.

JULIO: You're not inside my body! I hurt.

INES: I'm just here to help you. If you don't want to do anything for yourself, then stay the way you are. I'm going outside, it's hot in here. *(Starts to exit)*

JULIO: No. Wait!

INES: What?

JULIO: What are we going to do next?

INES: Walk.

JULIO *(Moves away)*: No walking. I told you, I'm not walking.

INES: You walked yesterday after the exercises.

JULIO: I can't today.

INES: Then I'm going outside to smoke!

JULIO: Ey, don't get angry!

INES: I just want your cooperation.

JULIO: I don't like pain. My whole body aches.

INES: It's going to hurt. What do you expect? You don't use your muscles. They're flaccid.

JULIO: I need nutrition. I need to get stronger. It takes time for the body to heal.

INES: Of course, I know that.

JULIO: So, it's not going to happen overnight!

(Pepe rides by on his bicycle. He rings the bell.)

INES: That's Pepe with the mail.

(Pepe parks the bicycle.)

Come in, Pepe.

PEPE: Good morning!

INES: Good morning.

JULIO: Morning.

PEPE *(To Julio)*: You don't look good. *(To Ines)* And you don't have a good face either. *(Puts his bag down)* What's wrong?

INES: What do you think happens in this house every day! (*Turns to Julio*)

JULIO: What do you mean? I don't always complain!

INES: You complain every day, Julio.

JULIO: I'm not an athlete. —She makes me exercise as if I was training for a tournament.

INES: He's exaggerating.

JULIO: Explain to her . . . tell her how I was a month ago. How I had tubes coming out of my mouth and IVs in both arms.

PEPE: So now you're better. What's wrong with exercising?

JULIO (*Moves away in the wheelchair*): Ah, the hell with you! You're just like her.

INES: He's mad because I added five repetitions to his exercises.

JULIO: She says it like it's nothing.

PEPE: Why don't you try helping her out? Pretend you're training for a sport. Baseball. It's not any different. If you have to run five laps, you run the five laps. You condition your mind to do it.

JULIO: When I played sports I wasn't sick.

PEPE: Here, mail for you. (*Goes through a bundle of mail*) You got a postcard from Venice. And you also got a letter from the Interior Ministry . . .

INES: Don't give it to him now. I'll take it. (*Grabs the mail*) He has to finish his exercises.

JULIO: Give me my mail! Let me see my postcard.

INES (*Gives him the postcard*): Here. The rest stays with me. If it's bad news you'll get in a rotten mood, and you won't do anything else. You still have to walk.

JULIO: What did she say?

PEPE: Come on, be a good sport. You have to cooperate. Be more hopeful, my friend.

JULIO: That's all I need—hope. What can I hope for?

PEPE: That's unlike you. You've turned into a lazy animal.

INES: Yes he has. He's turned into a hippopotamus that wants to stay in the water and do nothing for himself. —Don't look at me that way. I read a magazine article about the hippopotamus. *(Julio gives her a dirty look)* The hippos don't want to evolve. The penguin is an evolving animal. Penguins want to move forward. They're up on their feet and walking about. The seals, too. Those are evolving animals. But hippos want to stay in the water and do nothing for themselves. Just like Julio.

JULIO: You like to bother me, don't you? You like to bother me.

INES: No. I'm just not going to move from here until you walk.

PEPE: And neither am I.

(There is a pause. Julio looks at them in disbelief.)

INES: What are you doing on Sunday, Pepe? Do you want to go to the Botanical Gardens?

(Julio wheels himself to another part of the room.)

PEPE: What's at the Botanical Garden?

INES: There's a flowering tree from India I want to see. I was reading about it in the newspaper. This tree lives for two hundred years. It grows and grows for all these years, then it blooms once in its lifetime and dies away . . . It gives so many blooms that the weight of the flowers makes the tree bend down and fall to the ground.

PEPE: That sounds like a nice thing to do on Sunday, go see a tree.

JULIO: She also said, she wanted to talk to the tree, and sleep under it before it falls down. I have a lunatic in my house.

INES: So what's wrong with visiting a falling tree, Julio! I'm going outside to get the laundry, when I come back you'll take a walk! *(Starts to exit)*

JULIO: Give me the rest of my mail . . . give me my mail . . .

(Ines is gone now.)

She's not giving me my mail . . . She's mad, crazy . . .

(Pepe walks in Ines's direction. He contemplates her from a distance:)

PEPE: She's beautiful. Passionate. I love her . . . I remember the first day I saw her. She was trying to catch a canary that had gotten out of the cage. I just stood there and watched her make her way slowly to the bird, her hands full of seeds. After two minutes the bird couldn't resist her anymore and flew into her hands. Couldn't resist her, I tell you. I'd like to have a woman like her in my life.

JULIO: No you wouldn't. She's like a sergeant.

PEPE: Well, that's what you need. Somebody to get you back in shape.

JULIO: You're talking as if—

PEPE: Treat her well. You don't want to lose her. We found the right person to take care of you. She's hard-working, kind and determined. I'd marry her if I were in your shoes.

JULIO: What are you talking about? I'm a mess. Who's going to want to look at me in this condition?

PEPE: You never know. She's a good woman. I don't like to see you alone. I'd like to see you get married again. You deserve someone like Ines. She's a giving person. Nowadays a person calculates what they can afford to give . . . The world is changing, my friend. It's not how it used to be.

JULIO: Are you sure you're not the one who likes her?

PEPE: Me? Of course not! I can stay alone. I like my freedom. I like being alone.

JULIO: Have you tried getting back with Lolín?

PEPE: Lolín is gone, Julio. She's gone. She must be in America, for all I know. Got away on a raft. Didn't even say good-bye.

JULIO: Why not?

PEPE: Who knows with women! She wouldn't talk to me after we had that big fight.

JULIO: She probably thought you would turn her in for leaving the country.

PEPE *(With contained anger)*: Would I do that! Would I do something like that!

(Pause.)

Give me a cigarette, will you? You and I have rotten luck with women.

(Julio gives Pepe a cigarette.)

JULIO: When did she leave the country?

PEPE: I don't know, probably two or three weeks ago. —I didn't know she had left. Somebody told me.

JULIO: You're not taking this well, are you?

PEPE: No, I'm not. It's pointless. Why don't we talk about you?

JULIO: I have nothing to say. I feel rotten, like always.

PEPE: We should've left this place long ago. —Look at the two of us, alone again!

It's getting tough out there. You don't know how bad it is, because you never leave the house. But I can tell you, we're slowly going back to the Iron Age. We're in the Bicycle Age out there. We've gone back to the wheel. A whole country riding bicycles. You only have to look outside the window and see for yourself. Everywhere signs, slogans: SAVE ENERGY. SAVE ENERGY. What energy is there to be saved, when there is no energy! No oil. Hardly any buses running. I think this is the worst it's gotten in years. I mean last night the only thing I had to eat was an egg. I sat down to have dinner. I saw the miserable egg, in the middle of my plate looking at me, like an eyeball. The thing gave me the creeps. I mean it looked like it was hungrier than me . . . Just didn't have dinner at all, ran out of the house, got on my bicycle and went for some fresh air. I could feel my adrenaline going through my veins and up to my mouth. I think that's what filled my stomach last night, my own fuckin' anguish frothing on my tongue. —Do you know what I'm trying to do now? Did I tell you? I'm trying to learn Italian.

JULIO: Italian? Why do you want to learn Italian for?

PEPE: Sure. Why not? Learn a few words . . . I want to hook up with an Italian tourist. Imagine if I find an Italian woman. That would be my ticket out of this country. I'll get married, she'll send for me . . .

JULIO: Ah, give me a break. Do you really believe it's that easy?

PEPE: Why not? Even if I don't get to marry her, it's one way out of this mess.

JULIO: So who's teaching you Italian?

PEPE: Who's teaching me Italian, hunh?! Someone lent me this Italian sewing book. *(Takes out a small book from his pocket)*

JULIO: A sewing book. And what are you going to learn with an Italian sewing book?

PEPE: Oh, you should've seen me carrying on a conversation. I went to a bar and found an Italian woman and I said . . . listen to this . . .

(Pepe flips through the book and chooses a section. He enunciates every word with natural speed and mastery:)

"Questa giacca é strappata, desidero che mi sia rammendata." Tell me if that doesn't sound good!

JULIO: What does it mean?

PEPE: Can you sew a button on this coat for me?

JULIO: You told her that!

PEPE: Doesn't it sound good? Listen to this: "Desidero che mi si prendano le misure per un abito." That means I want to be measured.

JULIO: You're out of your mind.

PEPE: Ey . . . she thought it was amusing. I got her talking. I needed a punch line.

JULIO: Did she punch you back on the face?

PEPE: No. We had a good conversation. Then, she went to the bathroom, and I had three drinks waiting for her to come back.

JULIO: Did she come back?

PEPE: No. I spent all my money on drinks. Today I'm poor and shitting blood. I have an ulcer. I can't drink.

(Ines enters with a bundle of clothes wrapped in a white tablecloth. She places it on the table. She continues talking as she makes a couple of knots with the four corners of the tablecloth.)

INES: Did you hear me from out there? I was calling you to come out onto the patio. There was a whole flock of birds flying over the house. Hundreds of them. You can tell the season is changing. You can tell by the birds, they come here for the winter, then start making their way back North. —Are you almost ready, Julio? Have you had a chance to rest?

JULIO: I've already told you, it's enough for today.

INES: Did he tell you what the doctor said?

(Silence.)

PEPE: What's the matter, Julio?

INES: Julio, he's talking to you. *(To Pepe)* Was he always like this?

PEPE: No. I don't know what's gotten into him. He was always well disposed.

JULIO: I have to have surgery. *(To Ines)* Does that make you happy?

PEPE: What kind of surgery?

INES: I told him he should do it. It's the only way he's going to get cured.

JULIO: When I leave this place, I can have surgery. When I get my travel permit.

INES: When you get a travel permit! When you get a travel permit! You're going to have to wait a long time for a travel permit. You better find somebody with a boat and leave this place. If you wait too long, you're going to go pim-poom, right there and have another stroke!

JULIO *(To Pepe)*: Pim-poom . . . Everything is pim-poom to her! Everything happens in a matter of seconds.

INES: He could have another stroke, if he doesn't have surgery. That's what the doctor said.

JULIO: In her mind she has gotten a raft and sailed up North from this room.

PEPE: And why not, Julio?

INES: That's right. He knows he can't be waiting around. Do you know how long it takes to get a travel permit?!

JULIO: And where am I going to get a boat?

INES *(To Pepe)*: Can't you get somebody to build a raft? I told him I'll go with him. What's important is to go, leave this place.

PEPE: It's not impossible. We can get a raft.

JULIO: Then you two can get inside the raft because I'm not going anywhere. What if something happens, enh?

PEPE: Why do you always have to think of the worst!

JULIO: Because you only have to look at me sitting in this wheelchair! I can't do much for myself, goddamnit! I'm an invalid!

(Pause.)

Come on, let's go. Let's go . . . I'll take a walk.

INES *(Tenderly)*: Good. That's a good sport.

Pepe, as soon as I stand him up, you take the wheelchair and stand there where you are. Julio, you're going to walk to him.

JULIO: That's too far. Take two steps forward.

INES *(To Pepe)*: You stay where you are. *(To Julio)* Let's see, put your arms around me, as if we're going to dance.

PEPE: You want me to play music? *(Gets a radio)*
JULIO: Shut up will you! Don't be a clown.

(Julio stands up to walk. Pepe turns on the radio. A rumba plays.)

PEPE: Why not? You need something to liven you up.
INES: Don't drag your feet. Lift up your feet.

(Pepe moves the wheelchair out of Julio's reach and gets back to his place. The dialogue overlaps:)

JULIO: I'm trying. Turn that shit off!
INES: Lift up your leg.
PEPE: That's it, Julio . . .
JULIO: Turn that shit off! It doesn't let me concentrate!
PEPE: Bravo, Julio! Bravo! You're doing it!
INES: Push forward!
PEPE: Go, Julio! Go! Walk! To the finish line . . .
JULIO: Tell him to shut up!
INES: Shut up! Can't you see he's concentrating.
JULIO: Just tell him to put the chair behind me.
INES: No. You walk all the way to him.
PEPE: Go, Julio! Go!
JULIO: Bring the chair, big mouth!
INES: Don't do it, Pepe.
JULIO: Tell him to bring the chair.
INES: Let him finish turning around, Pepe.
PEPE: That's it . . . that's it, Julio. There you go. *(Ines lowers Julio down into the wheelchair)* Bravo, Julio . . . Bravo . . .

(Pepe goes to turn off the radio.)

INES: Are you all right?

(Pause. Julio catches his breath.)

JULIO: You want me to throw myself to the sea—look at me! How can I put myself in a little raft, on a truck tire, when I can't walk well enough? Can't you see I'm drowning! I'm sinking in my own body. I'm sitting here on solid ground and I'm drowning.

(Julio wheels himself out of the room. Pause. Ines looks at Pepe.)

PEPE *(Taking his bag)*: I'll come by later. *(Starts to exit)*
INES: Pepe, what is this thing that he has that won't let him move forward?

(The lights change.)

Scene 3

"Five Months Later" is projected on the screen. Five months have passed since the start of the play. Ines gets a sheet. She drapes it around Julio. She gives him a photo album. She gets a pair of scissors and starts cutting his hair. Julio flips through the photo album.

INES: How long ago was that? You look young in that picture.
JULIO: I was seventeen.
INES: And this guy standing by the seawall?
JULIO: Guess?
INES: Pepe. But it doesn't look like him.
JULIO: He was probably twelve. Look at him in shorts. He used to love the sea.
INES: And that doesn't look like you either . . . You look handsome with that mustache. You should grow one.
JULIO: Let me look in the mirror. Let me see what you're doing.
INES: No. Not until I'm finished. I still have to cut your sideburns. Who are those people wearing sunglasses, in that picture?

JULIO: That's me and Ana María. She was feeding the pigeons in the park.

INES: Let me see. You still love this woman, don't you?

JULIO: That was the past.

INES: I know when she's on your mind. I've seen your eyes water . . . I know you well enough. I've worked in this house for five months now. The only thing left is to pin myself to your skin. Sometimes I feel like I am your body, and you are my brain.

JULIO: I don't want to talk about her.

INES: Then cut her out of your mind, like I cut your hair. She's not coming back, and thinking about her won't do any good. It's just like those pills you take, when you get depressed—she doesn't go away with pills. She left you. She could've taken care of you.

JULIO: Ines, please . . .

INES: I just see you sad-eyed sometimes . . .

JULIO: Now come on, that's none of your business.

INES: You are my business. You're my work. That's why I come to this house every morning.

JULIO: But we're not married.

INES: Ha! That I know.

JULIO: Good. Is that all you have to say?

INES: Yes.

JULIO: Then that's enough! Please, just get on with the haircut!

(She continues to cut his hair. Silence. The sound of Pepe's bicycle bell.)

That must be Pepe with the mail. He'll cough now. He always does.

(Pepe coughs. Julio and Ines laugh.)

PEPE: Good morning!

JULIO AND INES: Morning . . .

PEPE: What are you two laughing about?

JULIO: I was telling Ines that I know when you're here by the cough.

PEPE *(Taking off his bag)*: Well, at least this ship won't get lost in the fog. —It looks good, Julio. *(To Ines)* You do a good job. Can I be next?

JULIO: This is not a barbershop.

PEPE: She's good at it. I need a haircut.

INES: Today is Julio's birthday.

PEPE: I know. Happy birthday! Here. *(Throws him a pack of cigarettes)* I got you a pack of French cigarettes for your birthday.

INES: I'm giving him my present later this afternoon. It's a surprise.

JULIO: Thank you, Pepe.

PEPE: How old are you?

(Ines undrapes Julio.)

JULIO: Ancient. Old. —Let me look at myself in the mirror. Pass me the mirror.

INES: You stand up and get it.

JULIO: I guess no one is cordial anymore.

INES: That's right. We're mean and awful people.

(Julio gets up to get the mirror.)

See how well he's doing. See how good he looks.

PEPE *(Applauds)*: Bravo, Julio . . . bravo.

JULIO: I'm getting there.

INES: I told him we should go to the seawall and get some fresh air. I told him we should have a party.

JULIO: That's for kids who like birthday parties. I'm too old to be celebrating my birthday. *(Takes a small lamp out of the trunk)* I want you to sell this lamp, Pepe. I need money. I want to pay Ines.

INES: That's a beautiful lamp. You don't have to sell it to pay me.

PEPE: Aren't you getting paid at the end of the month?

JULIO: No more payments. They want me back at work. They say I'm capable of working at the office. —How much do you think we can get for it?

(He lights the lamp. The light reveals a painting on the lamp shade.)

PEPE: I don't know. It's an old lamp. I can never estimate the price of old things.

INES: Don't sell it, Julio. Things get passed on in our families and we take them for granted. But these objects have a life. They become part of the family. They've lived with us.

JULIO: Like this lamp, Pepe, she's my cousin.

INES: I'm not saying anything else! It's your house, those are your objects . . . you do what you want! *(To Pepe)* He knows he doesn't have to pay me. I can get by until he gets back to work.

JULIO *(Gives Pepe an old silver pot)*: Here. Take this too. How much can we get for this?

INES: That's silver. Don't sell that.

JULIO: I don't use it. How much?

PEPE: You won't get much money for it . . . I could exchange it for food, a couple of chickens.

INES: Get a tire. Exchange everything for a tire. Let's build a raft and get out of this place!

(There is a pause. Julio stares at Ines. She was so direct in her response, it's as if her mind had spoken before she could come up with the words.)

It's not going to get any better here. Every day more and more slogans. The permanent war: CONTRIBUTE . . . RESISTANCE . . . DO IT FOR YOUR COUNTRY . . . Every day the same story, no room for questioning. They take away your food and they tell you: "Keep on going." "You can go on." Call this moving, call it going on?

The spirit of the system . . . They take away the fuel, no more buses . . . Now a bicycle, just ride it. Call it a bicycle to take you to the sea, fresh air . . . That's it. You have adopted the right spirit towards things . . .

Only one dress to wear, call it one dress for a year. A year for a dress . . . A dress without a year. I'm tired of fooling myself. —If you don't want to leave this place, I do! I do! You can give me a raft for payment!

(Silence. She doesn't know what else to say, and Julio doesn't know how to respond.)

I'm going outside for some fresh air.

(Pepe tries to make light of the whole situation. He drapes himself with the sheet. He sits on the chair. Ines starts to leave.)

PEPE: Aren't you going to give me a haircut?

(Ines ignores him, she continues out.)

Does this mean she's not going to give me a haircut? What happened, Julio? Where is she going? *(In a loud voice)* Eh, I'm ready for the haircut.

(She's out of the house.)

(To Julio) Is she coming back? *(In a loud voice)* Ines . . . Ines . . .

(Pepe goes out of the house, still draped in the sheet. Ines takes his bicycle.)

Hey . . . come back . . . come back . . .

(Pepe enters the house.)

She took my bicycle.

(A bolero plays. The lights change.)

Scene 4

"Later in the Evening" is projected on the screen. The men are waiting for Ines outside the house. Ines rides in on the bicycle, ringing the bicycle bell several times, expressing joy and excitement. She has a package.

INES: I'm back. I'm back . . .
PEPE: I was getting worried. Next time tell me where you're going.
INES: I didn't take long. Come inside. Close your eyes, Julio.
JULIO: What for? What's this all about?
INES: Just close your eyes. I have a surprise for you. Come on . . . come on . . . close your eyes.

(Julio closes his eyes. She leads him into the house. She places a box on his lap.)

Open your eyes.

(Julio opens the box. It's a radio.)

Yours doesn't work well, and this one is portable. Now you can listen to the news all day. *(Kisses him on the forehead)*
JULIO: Why did you do this? You don't have to give me a present.
INES: Happy birthday! Let's have a drink. *(Takes out a bottle of rum. Goes for three glasses and pours)* Find a good station on the radio. We'll have to toast. Say something, Pepe!

PEPE: To . . . to Julio del Valle. To many . . . many more. That didn't
sound good. I want to say something brilliant.

INES: To his health! And next year in another land.

PEPE: Yes, why not? All of us somewhere else. Somewhere else . . .
Good appetite! Isn't that what the French say?

INES: Something like that.

PEPE: Then grand, big, good appetite. Appetite to eat a whole cow
to you, Julio.

(They toast:)

JULIO: Salud . . .

INES AND PEPE: Salud . . .

INES: We'll have to dance.

JULIO: No, no, no, no . . .

INES: Come on and dance with me.

(Ines pulls Julio to dance.)

JULIO: Dance with *him.*

INES: You have to dance.

JULIO: I can't dance. I don't know how to dance.

INES: Oh come on!

JULIO: No . . . no dancing . . .

INES: You're lying. You can dance.

JULIO: You're crazy. I don't want to dance.

INES: Well, I won't force you. I'll leave you alone because it's your
birthday.

(Pause.)

I went real far to get this rum. I know this is the one you
like. I wanted this day to be special.

JULIO *(Pours more rum in her glass)*: You want more, Pepe?

PEPE: Sure. *(Toasting)* To your health! We would all like something better. Life is like that. We all want something better.
—See, I'm getting better at this.

(They drink.)

INES: Play music, Pepe. We'll dance. Oh, I can feel the rum rising
to my face.

*(Pepe switches on the radio. An old bolero plays, something like
"Veinte Años.")*

Leave that song on! I love old music. I used to collect music
like this one. Oh! I collected all kinds of things . . . Oh! So
many things gone. Got rid of everything . . . all of it gone . . .
(Dances by herself) Gave everything away . . . I thought I was
going to leave this place. But it never happened.

(The rum makes her giddy. She laughs.)

I was stupid. Gone mad in the head. And all for a German
tourist. With him I went to all the nightclubs. I wore sunglasses and pretended to be a foreigner. All the waiters
thought I was from Brazil, Italy, Portugal, until the German
would get stuck ordering something, and I would have to
open my mouth. *(Laughs at herself)* He was gone at the end
of summer . . . August . . . September . . . gone away . . .
(Becomes bitter) Like all foreigners, they leave when the
seaweed comes to the shores. The scum of the sea. He left
dressed the same way I met him, starched white shirt . . . I
stayed a mess, a shipwreck . . . *(Determined)* Oh, I'd like to
live in a place where the land extends and I can walk for
miles, where I can run and never reach the end.

   Here, there's always the sea. The jail of water. Stagnant.
Just the sea. —Oh, this rum is going to my head, Pepe.

(She stops dancing and goes to the table.)

Are you happy, Julio? Are you happy on your birthday?

JULIO: I'm as happy as can be.

INES: That's the most important thing, for you to be happy. Drink with me! Drink, Pepe! Drink some more!

(She pours more rum in their glasses.)

JULIO: No, that's too much.

PEPE: Drink up . . . drink up . . .

INES: That's it, drink . . . oh, I want to dance again. Let's dance.

PEPE: No. No dancing. No more dancing . . .

(Pepe switches off the radio.)

JULIO: Let's just sit. Let's just sit and talk.

(The rum is lightening Ines's spirit now, but she's not drunk.)

INES: Can you drink a lot, Pepe? Can you drink a lot without getting drunk?

JULIO: Oh, he can drink like a fish. I've seen him drunk more than a couple of times.

(The men laugh.)

INES: I can't drink. *(Lifts up her glass)* It all goes to my head, it opens my mouth and I talk too much. That's why I never drink. We talk too much, period. We are too loud and loose with our tongues.

JULIO: And what's wrong with that? What's wrong with talking?

INES: We should measure our words, like the English.

PEPE: If I do that, then I wouldn't speak my mind. If you measure your words, then you don't really say what you feel inside.

INES *(Sits down)*: I think the Germans are like the English. They can talk to you about their deepest sorrows and still keep their calm . . . The German man, he was always talking about politics. He was always arguing whether we had gotten stuck because of the Americans or the Russians, whether we would survive all alone in the middle of the sea.

JULIO: Probably saw the worst year we had. The first year the Russians abandoned us . . . We were all like ants, running here and there. Wondering what would happen next.

INES: —Oh, I don't like talking about politics. To me wars seem useless and unreasonable. Destruction. God destroys, but his destruction is always justified. He destroys in perfect order. He's an artist at it. After his hurricanes and earthquakes, there's always a blue morning with clouds. And if there's rain, it's because he hasn't finished cleaning up after himself. But we haven't learned to master that art. Man is sloppy and messy, and he can never master that art.

(There are tears in her eyes. She is lost in memory, her own destruction swelling in her throat.)

Oh, why couldn't I leave this place! What's the use of staying in one place for so long?

(She lowers her head to her arms. Julio looks at her full of love and affection. He reaches out to her. Pepe remains quiet and still. He looks at them. The lights change.)

Scene 5

"Ten Days after Julio's Birthday, October 11, 1993" is projected on the screen. Sound of rain and thunder. The stage is dimly lit. There are folded sheets and pillowcases on top of the table. Ines sits at the table, mending a pillowcase. Julio stands next to her.

JULIO: Pepe came by late last night and I gave him a few things to sell. I gave him a vase and some old jewelry I had.

INES: You're selling everything, Julio. The house is starting to look sad.

JULIO: That's all right.

INES: You're not going to sell these, are you? I'm mending them.

JULIO: No. I did give him some more old frames and silverware. I told him to get what we need to go out to sea.

INES: Does this mean—oh, Julio!

JULIO: Yes, I'm ready to do it. I'm ready to plunge myself into the sea. What do I have to lose?

INES: Oh, Julio! *(Embraces him)* So? So?

JULIO: He's going to find somebody to build a raft.

INES: When is it going to be ready? When are we leaving?

JULIO: Calm down. We still have to find more things.

INES: Is Pepe coming?

JULIO: Yes he is.

INES *(Hugs him)*: Oh, Julio . . .

(There's an awkward moment as their bodies touch.)

JULIO: Is there food?

INES: Yes. There's soup left from last night.

JULIO: Shouldn't we turn on the lights? You're going to hurt your eyes.

INES: It's not that bad, I can see. The rain brings a light of its own and I like sewing in this light. The rain makes me do things I don't normally do. It makes me sit down like an old woman and do this. Look at this pillowcase . . . The string got pulled out, and you can't make out the initials. The D looks like a C backwards.

JULIO: All that linen is falling apart. They've been in the family for so long.

INES: I know it's old. But it's still beautiful. Who knows how many generations! How many heads have slept on this pillowcase. I was just imagining all the women in your family, who slept on this pillowcase.

I like your last name. I've always liked last names that begin with the letter D: del Campo, del Valle, de las Casas, de los Angeles. It makes one's name seem more regal. It makes you feel as if you belong to something, of this, of that. It just flows like history.

I want to lay my head on this pillowcase. Close to you.

(She looks at him. They embrace.)

I love you, Julio.

(They embrace again.)

I want us to forget who we are. Start a new life away from here. Let's forget who we are.

(She kisses him on the forehead. Then she takes the pillowcase and gently tries to cover his face. Gentle guitar music plays.)

JULIO: What are you doing?
INES: A game. Just a game to start a new life. Just let me do it. Look at me. When we lift up the cloth we'll start a new life.

(Julio lets his face be covered by the pillowcase. Now Ines covers her own face with a pillowcase. Julio touches her face through the cloth. He brings her close to him. They kiss through the pillowcases. The sound of the sea fills the stage. Blackout.)

AGUA

Scene 1

"Agua: The Sea" is projected on the screen. Blue lights. Sounds of the wind and sea fill the stage. On a raft in the middle of the Caribbean Sea, Ines and Pepe are rowing. Julio is standing, facing upstage with a compass in his hand.

PEPE: A good-for-nothing, I tell you. A miserable-wretched-mind-blind-deplorable beast. You can ask Julio what it took to get food, a piece of meat out of that moron.

JULIO: Yes, she was an imbecile.

PEPE: It took bidding didn't it?

JULIO: Persuasion, eh! The imbecile wouldn't take anything.

INES: This rowing is getting to me, Pepe.

PEPE: Don't think about it. —I said to the mountain woman, "What does it take to do an exchange? You give me a few pounds of jerked beef and I give you this radio. Good con-

dition. The radio plays music like an orchestra. Long
antenna. Picks up northern stations at night . . . western
stations, eastern stations, as far as Vienna." I even told her
that I had danced to Viennese waltzes at night, and all from
the radio. And what did the moron say, Julio?

JULIO: "No. No love. No music."

INES: What did she mean by that?

JULIO: I said to her, "Love yes, much love. You sitting on a horse
riding through the prairies, playing the radio."

PEPE: Yes. Then he told her, "Jerked beef for us, radio for you . . .
radio for love."

JULIO: And the moron started to laugh, and she said, "Hee . . . hee
. . . Love . . . No love . . . hee . . . hee . . . A scratch . . . a scratch
in my heart . . . My big sister stole my love."

PEPE: I felt sad when she said that . . .

JULIO: Let me finish, Pepe . . . She said, "Maybe radio for crying."
But then she said, "No . . . no . . . If I cry, Mama will holler
at me." That's when she told us to go to Adolfina, that she
had fat chickens and lots of jerked beef.

    Then I saw the mountain woman looking at Pepe's bicy-
cle and I pulled him aside and told him, "I bet you anything
that if you give her the bicycle, she'll give us the ten pounds
of jerked beef." And wasn't I right?

PEPE: Yes, you were.

JULIO: I said to him, "Even if we have to walk ten miles, we're not
going anywhere without getting the jerked beef."

INES: Is this it?

JULIO: Yes. We figured it's the only thing that wouldn't spoil.

PEPE: Do you think we're on the northeastern current? Roberto
said that when we reach the straits of Florida, the current
flows eastward. Are we still moving towards the northeast?

JULIO (*Looks at compass*): If this compass is any good, it looks like
we're moving north. (*To Pepe*) What does it look like to you?

PEPE: Yes we're moving northeast.

INES: Are you sure we're not moving towards the northwest? —
Which way is east?

PEPE (*Points to the left, then the right, then makes up a new direction*): This way. No, this way. This way. This thing can't
make up its mind. It doesn't like pointing north now.

INES: I don't see the current moving us to the east or to the west.
I just see waves. How can you tell the current is moving
eastwards? How can you see in this darkness?

JULIO: The compass, Ines. The compass.

INES: I've been rowing for more than five hours and it feels like
we haven't moved a bit. That thing doesn't work. Look at
what happened to Columbus, he wanted to go to India and
ended up in the Bahamas and Puerto Rico.

PEPE: We can't even see the city lights. Of course we're moving.

INES (*Stands up and looks at the seascape*): I can. I can still see the
shimmering lights.

JULIO: Where?

INES: Back that way.

PEPE: That must be the reflection of the moon on the water.

INES: It feels as if we're inside the mouth of a wolf.

JULIO: A whale.

(*Pepe takes up rowing.*)

PEPE: Let's get to it, Ines: One, two . . . one, two . . . (*Continues to
count between the lines*)

JULIO: Take a break.

PEPE (*Continues rowing*): We have to pass the picket line! We have
to pass the picket line!

INES: How do we know when we pass the picket line?

PEPE: There'll be ships, American coast guards. Balloons . . .

INES: Will they be able to see us in the dark?

PEPE: There'll be thousands of ships, people waving at us. Come
on, one, two . . . one, two . . . one, two . . . one, two . . .

INES: Take a break. I can't rest if I see you rowing. I start feeling
    guilty.

JULIO: Take a break!

PEPE *(Stops rowing and lies back)*: Give me a cigarette, Julio.

(Silence.)

INES: I don't know about you but I'm afraid. I get this bad feeling
    in my heart. Ay, I start to think that we'll end up drowned!

PEPE AND JULIO: Ines!

INES *(Covers her ears)*: No . . . I didn't say that. Tell me you didn't
    hear me say that. *(Uncovers her ears)* But I had to say it.

JULIO: That's why we have to keep our minds away from those
    thoughts. We have to think about other things.
        When I was in the military, one time we got lost—for days
    stranded in the wild, under the scorching sun. We just could-
    n't find our way back to camp. And I used to tell myself, We're
    getting there . . . we're getting there. I'd repeat it over and
    over again in my mind. I would picture the city, the streets,
    the buildings, and that's what kept me going.

INES: What we need is a nightcap, something to put us to sleep.
    I just never thought that water could be so frightening.

JULIO: It is frightening.

INES: All this darkness.

PEPE: I've never seen so many stars.

INES: And look at their reflection on the waves. You can't even
    tell if the stars belong to the night or the sea. It makes me
    want to fish them out of the water. —Give me something
    to drink, Julio.

JULIO: We have to save the water.

INES: I've been rowing for five hours I need some water.

PEPE: He's just trying to save the water. If we run out of water
    we're in bad shape. Remember what Robertico said, no
    matter what happens we can't drink salt water.

JULIO: You guys are going to have to turn around. I have to take a leak.

INES: Yes, I've been wondering how I'm going to pee, because you guys can just pull out your thing. I'm afraid of sticking out my butt and getting bitten by a shark. I've seen a few circling us.

PEPE: So have I. I just didn't want to say anything. They've been following us for some time.

JULIO: So aren't you going to turn around?

(Pepe and Ines turn around. Pause.)

INES: Well?

JULIO: Give me a second, will you!

(Pause.)

INES: Did you finish?

JULIO: I can't do it.

INES: How come?

JULIO: I can't pee when there are people around me. It takes me longer.

INES: You better get used to us.

PEPE: Listen to the water, it will make you want to pee.

INES: Pssssssssssssssssssssssssssssssssssssssssssssss . . .

JULIO: What are you doing?

INES: That's what my mother used to do when my brother couldn't pee.

JULIO: Forget it. I'll pee later.

INES: You better get used to us.

JULIO: I will. I'll pee later.

INES: Why don't you play some music from the little radio? If we get an American station we'll know we're moving north.

PEPE *(Switches on the radio)*: No American stations.

INES: See, who knows where we're heading, we can't even get a northern station! You're not a seaman and neither is he and I don't know anything about the sea, except it's a good place to cry.

JULIO: Give me a cigarette, Pepe. It's going to be a long night.

INES: Give me one, too. Being in the middle of nowhere makes us nervous. Not enough room to walk. Not enough space to run. I know I won't be able to sleep tonight.

JULIO: Me neither.

PEPE: That makes three of us. I have a hard time sleeping on land.

INES: You can't find a damn station?

JULIO: No.

INES: I want to hear an American song to make me feel we're getting closer. Billie Holiday, so I can have good cry and calm myself. Don't get mad at me, Julio. I feel like crying.

(A Cuban bolero plays, something like "Lágrimas Negras." Ines moves to the rhythm.)

Leave that station on . . . Paranh . . . pan . . . pan . . . pan . . . panh . . .

JULIO: Don't sing. Control yourself. You're making the raft move.

INES: Let me sing . . . I feel like singing . . .

(Ines sings. The men join in. Ines gets a spoon and makes music with a metal cup. Pepe uses the wood on the raft as a drum. The sound of the ocean swells as the lights dim. The sound of the waves increases, drowning out the music. Silence. The lights change.)

Scene 2

"Second Day Out at Sea" is projected on the screen. Ines coughs. Julio holds a bottle of water. Pepe is asleep.

JULIO: Drink some water.

INES: This thirst is getting to me. My mouth fills up with a bitter foam.

JULIO: Have some more water.

(Ines takes a drink.)

INES: That's enough. I was having a bad dream. I was thirsty as a dry lake and my left breast was overflowing with water. But I couldn't drink, because I couldn't bring my mouth close enough to my chest. But you came close to me and sucked the water from my breast and gave me some water to drink. And I couldn't stop drinking from your mouth from my breast, because the thirst was insatiable. I drank and drank water. The more I drank, the more water flowed out my breast. And I couldn't stop and neither could you. If you stopped giving me water, the flow would stop. And it felt like I had enough to quench a desert. Just thinking about it gives me a strange sensation, as if I had water in there. *(Brings her hand to her breast)*

JULIO: Come here . . . *(She moves close to him)* Closer . . . Closer . . .

(She squats over his legs. He starts unbuttoning her dress.)

INES: What are you doing?

JULIO: Shshshh . . . I want to see your breasts.

INES: Here Julio? In the middle of the sea with Pepe next to us?!

JULIO: Yes . . .

(He pulls her close to him. He starts kissing her breasts and her neck.)

INES: No. You're insane.

JULIO: Why? Come here. I need to drink from you.

INES: But it was a dream.

JULIO *(Unzipping his fly)*: Dreams become real.

INES: No. Stop it.

JULIO: Why not? I want to taste you.

INES: We'll wake him up.

JULIO: Stay like this on top of me. We don't have to move, the sea is already moving. Stay like that, like that.

INES: No, Julio.

JULIO *(Kissing her)*: Yes, stay there.

INES: We'll wake him up.

(She starts to give in.)

JULIO: No, this could be the last time.

INES: Don't say that!

JULIO: Yes. What if we never make it, my love?

INES: We'll make it.

JULIO: Stay like this as if it were the last time.

INES: We'll make it. Don't say we won't make it.

JULIO: If we don't make it, we can say we did it one last time. I was inside you one last time. One last time.

INES: Why are you so stubborn!

JULIO: Because you make me stubborn. Your skin, your face, having you so close to me, knowing that at any moment life could end for me.

INES: No, not for you. Nothing will happen to you while I'm here. Even if death comes near us I would let it take me first.

JULIO *(Reaching an orgasm)*: Oh, Ines . . . Ines . . . Ines . . .

INES: Ay, Julio!

(He leans back.)

JULIO: You see there was water inside you, like rain.

(She embraces him. They lie down together on the raft. The sound of the sea fills the stage. The lights change.)

Scene 3

"Third Day Out at Sea" is projected on the screen. Julio and Ines are asleep. Pepe speaks to the sea. He's on top of the sail, looking out at the distance. He is hallucinating.

PEPE: If your voice is coming from there, say something! *(Pause)* If your voice is coming from there, say something! *(Pause)* Push me! Push me, like you said you would.

(The sound of children laughing—a distant angelic aria. Then the continual sound of the rippling waves.)

Don't think you can play with my mind! You can't trick me. You're not going to make me lose my head. I'm not sentimental. I'm not. I'm like a fish. Scales. Sharp bones. You never see a fish cry.

Why cry, when fish live in the water?

If I cry, I'll cry in the shower, enh! So no one can see my tears. Tears to the water. Water to the sea.

(The sound of the roaring sea. The sound of a child calling someone in the distance. Then it all subsides. Silence.)

I've heard what the ocean does to people. I've heard. Like the desert. A fever. You see things. A mirage. You play tricks on the eyes.

What ever became of that day, eh? What ever became of that day when I was a child, and my father brought the whole family together and said, "We're moving to the coast, and I'm going to show you the sea." And we sold all the chickens to buy the bus fare. We sold the cows and the pigs to rent a house close to the seashore.

Look . . . look . . . You can't trick me! I can close my eyes . . . I can close my eyes and see you like that first day, when the driver said, "We're in Havana. We're by the seawall." And I climbed down from the bus, with my eyes closed, and my father said, "Open your eyes, Pepe. Open your eyes. This is the sea. This is the sea." And when I saw you, you were blue and big as the falling sky. Calm and full as a bowl of blue soup . . . You were all I imagined you to be.

Look . . . look . . . look at me running to you. (*Starts running in place*) Look at me running to drink you! Look! Look! You can't trick me! (*The sound of children laughing*) You can't trick me! You're not a lie! You're not a lie! You're not a lie! You're not a lie! Look at me swimming! Look at me swimming! Look at me walking on your water—like Jesus. Julio! Ines! I'm walking on top of the sea like Jesus! (*The sound of a woman laughing in the distance*)

(*Julio and Ines wake up.*)

JULIO (*Half asleep*): One can't even . . .
PEPE (*Still running in place*): I'm walking . . .
INES: Pepe, what's gotten into you!
PEPE: I'm walking . . . I'm walking on top of the sea like Jesus.
INES: Stop that, Pepe! He's hallucinating, Julio! Grab him! Stop it! Stop! You're going to turn over the raft. (*Tries to make Pepe stop, tries to pull him down*)

(*The sound of children laughing in the distance.*)

PEPE: I'm walking! I'm getting there!

INES: Stop it!

JULIO: Stop it, Pepe! Stop it! STOP!

(Silence. Pepe is transfixed.)

PEPE: I'm thirsty.

INES: I am, too. Are you all right?

PEPE: My mind . . . I . . . I thought . . .

INES: Yes, Pepe . . .

PEPE: I saw things . . . The sea . . . I thought . . . I thought . . . My mind . . . it left me . . .

(The sound of loud thunder. The lights change.)

Scene 4

FUEGO (FIRE)

"Fourth Day Out at Sea" is projected on the screen. Sunset. Orange lights. Each character is in his own world. The sound of bongo drums. Spotlight on Julio looking at the sea. He is peeing into a metal cup.

JULIO: Nothing but water and no water to drink . . . I'm in the fuckin' middle of nowhere . . . I must think of cities and streets, fountains of sweet water . . . I'm starting to smell like codfish . . . sardines . . . No, mustn't try to think of those things . . . *(Closes his eyes)*

It's raining inside me and the rain flows downwards from the mountains, to the valleys . . . and the water is so pure that women wash their hair and let their children bathe . . .

(Julio takes a swig of urine.
Spotlight on Pepe looking up at the sky.)

177

PEPE: If I close my eyes . . . if I empty my mind and calm myself maybe sleep will come . . . maybe sleep will come . . . I'm in the middle of nowhere . . .

(Spotlight on Ines, looking at the sea.)

INES: No, mustn't have bad thoughts . . . I always wanted to leave. Always wanted to go . . . Now I have in front of me, the sea . . . the sea . . . I finally got to go . . .

(The spotlights fade. Dim orange light washes the stage.)

JULIO: If I close my eyes . . .
PEPE: If I calm myself . . .
INES: If I think of nothing . . .
JULIO: If I think of land, sweet water.
PEPE: I have to tell myself . . .
JULIO: Land . . .
PEPE: . . . that this is all a dream . . .
INES: Maybe sleep will come . . .
JULIO: Maybe sleep will come . . .
INES: It will come.
PEPE: I have to tell myself . . .
INES: I have to tell myself . . .
JULIO: I have to tell myself . . .
INES: the sea is my hammock, my hammock . . .
JULIO *(Abruptly)*: We're in the fuckin' middle of nowhere! How the hell did we get into all this rice and mangoes?

(The sound of bongo drums stops. Full lights.)

INES *(Hallucinating)*: Somebody is waving at me.
JULIO: Who?
INES: There . . .
PEPE: Wave back . . . *(In a loud voice)* Hello!

INES: Hello . . .

JULIO: There's nobody there . . . It's the sea . . . just the sea . . .

INES: It's not the sea . . . Somebody is waving at me . . .

JULIO: Nothing but water. It's our minds . . .

PEPE: Our minds? . . . Your mind . . . Not my mind—I like my mind.

INES *(In a loud voice)*: Hello out there! *(Waves. Opens an umbrella to attract attention. Squints, looks into the distance)* Hello out there! Hello!

(Pause.)

JULIO: See . . . No answer . . .

INES: What's the matter, you're jealous? Hello, out there!

PEPE: It's not a man. It's a woman . . .

JULIO: There's nobody out there, get that straight. Let's go to sleep, it's getting dark. When morning comes . . . when the sun rises . . . it will all be blue again . . .

PEPE: And we'll see rooftops at last . . .

INES: Windows . . .

JULIO: "Windows," she says! We're in the middle of nowhere.

INES: A sewing machine . . . When the wind blows gently I hear a sewing machine . . .

JULIO: She keeps seeing gondolas and sewing machines . . .

PEPE: Are you sure it's not a train? I keep hearing a train.

JULIO: She said a sewing machine, and now you—

PEPE: Then somebody is out there sewing . . .

JULIO *(Looks at Pepe in disbelief)*: Oh God.

INES: Yes, sewing, sewing, Julio . . .

JULIO: Sewing what?

PEPE: Handkerchiefs . . . white handkerchiefs to wave at us . . . Somebody is out there waiting for us . . .

JULIO *(Gives up on the whole thing)*: I'm going to sleep.

INES: I'm still going to keep an eye on my suitcase.

JULIO: What suitcase?

INES: A man took it to the end of the platform . . .

JULIO: What platform? What's the matter with you! It's the sea . . .
I keep telling you . . . Put this in your head . . .

PEPE *(Trying to explain to her)*: Yes and every time . . . What he's saying is that every time . . . every time we see something . . .

JULIO: Yes, tell her . . .

PEPE: What he's saying is that every time . . . every time we see
something . . .

JULIO *(Applauds, waiting to hear something brilliant)*: That's it . . .
Finally . . .

PEPE *(Puffing himself)*: Every time . . . every time we're getting
somewhere, it's just like another time without getting anywhere. Right, Julio? . . .

JULIO: Bravo . . .

(Pepe turns away and looks at the sky.)

PEPE: Then one more night to add to the list, till the next night . . .
Then the moon again . . . *(Looking at the moon now)* Same
old glare . . . *(Points up)* One more night with the moon . . .
And there she is again wearing white gloves, green slippers,
reeking of perfume, smoking her cigarette . . . and I have to
tell her, "Why do you do this to me?! . . . Why are you dressing up for me?! Why are you trying to fool me?! . . . Let me
go, enh. Let me go. Just let me be . . . " And I have to say, *(In
a loud voice, confused now)* "Is there anyone out there who
knows what's happening!"

JULIO: What is he saying now?

(For a moment Ines is back to reality. She closes her umbrella.)

INES: I don't know what he's saying.

JULIO: What are you saying? What are you saying? Who are you
talking to?

(Pause. Pepe continues to look at the sky, waiting for an answer. Ines looks up, full of hope.)

INES: He's talking to the moon.

JULIO: He's talking to the moon . . . *(To Pepe)* You better pull yourself together.

PEPE *(In a trance)*: Something has happened, Julio . . . You hear?

(Pause.)

JULIO: Nothing has happened . . . nothing . . .

PEPE: Yes something has happened and the world has gone away. There's nobody to talk to . . . nobody to ask.

(Ines sees something in the distance. She's hallucinating again.)

INES: Ask the man who is waving at me. Julio doesn't like him, but he's still waving at me.

JULIO: There isn't any man and there isn't any moon!

PEPE: Then we're fucked.

JULIO: You both are scaring the shit out of me . . . We're in the middle of nowhere and you're talking nonsense . . .

INES *(Gently)*: When the sun rises, it will be over, Julio. I keep seeing a bridge in my dreams. A white bridge, curved like a fallen halo in the middle of the sea.

PEPE *(Laughs with joy)*: When the sun rises I'll wash and shave my face like before . . .

INES *(Full of joy)*: And I'll walk into my balcony and water my geraniums . . . How about you, Julio?

(Julio finds relief; he starts to laugh.)

JULIO: Me . . . Oh I wish I could have a cigarette . . .

PEPE *(With an imaginary cigarette)*: Yes, smoke in your mouth, like before. Look at me, smoke in the air taking us back to your

house, your table. Opening the windows to let in seven
o'clock . . .

INES: Ah yes, seven o'clock! That's the time I like to get up. The
smell of seven o'clock . . . The oleanders by my window . . .

PEPE: Coffee . . .

INES: Moist leaves . . .

JULIO: Mist . . . Bread . . .

PEPE: Barbershops . . .

INES: Clocks ringing . . .

JULIO: Beds being made . . . And light making its way under door-
ways . . .

INES (*Suddenly seeing an imaginary airport*): You must tell those
men to be careful with my suitcase, Julio . . . (*To an imaginary person*) —Be careful. That blue suitcase has never gone
anywhere. It's liable to get lost—doesn't know of farewells
and train windows, people waving good-bye . . . (*To Pepe
and Julio*) Ay, you don't know how much I wanted a picture
sitting on top of my suitcase!

PEPE: I'm thirsty, Julio . . . Give me some water . . .

JULIO: We don't have any water.

PEPE: You drank it?

JULIO: Me? (*Lost for words*) We . . . You know well . . . We didn't
have any more . . .

PEPE: But there was . . . I saw it . . . we had . . . I saw it with my
eyes . . . Where's the bottle?

INES: What bottle?

(*Pepe starts searching for the bottle, making a mess.*)

PEPE (*Simultaneously*): It was full . . .

JULIO (*Simultaneously*): I didn't take any water . . .

PEPE: Where is it? Where is it? Where did you hide it?

INES: Where did you see it?

PEPE: I saw it . . . It was full.

INES: I didn't drink it.

PEPE: Someone drank it.

JULIO: I didn't drink it.

PEPE: Then who did? Who was it? Give it to me . . . You're hiding it—

JULIO: I'm not hiding anything . . .

PEPE: Give it to me . . . *(Grabs Julio by the shirt)* You took it. He has it! He has it! Give it to me . . .

(Pepe notices he has lost control. Pause. He lets go of Julio. He looks down at the waves. Silence.)

(Softly) I'm sorry . . . I'm . . . Something has happened, and I don't know what it is . . . I don't know who I am, what to do, what I've done—what's happening, Julio? What's happening? What's happening to me?

JULIO: Calm down.

INES *(Softly)*: You are Pepe, that's who you are . . . And . . . and I am Ines . . . You are Pepe, and I love you like I love Julio. *(Touches Pepe's face)* How can you forget who you are? How can you forget?

JULIO: Let's go to sleep. Tomorrow we'll be a little bit closer.

PEPE: Oh God . . . Now . . . I . . . I . . . now . . . now . . . Julio. She . . . she . . . Did you hear what she said?

JULIO: Let's go to sleep . . .

INES: But I love . . . *(Reaches out to Pepe)*

JULIO *(To Ines)*: Leave him alone.

PEPE *(Looking at Ines)*: Why?

JULIO *(To Ines)*: Leave him alone.

PEPE: Didn't you hear what she said?

JULIO: Let's go to sleep. We are weak. We are weak and tired, and we don't know what we're doing. We don't know what we're saying.

PEPE (*Full of joy, he shakes Julio*): But she says she loves me, Julio.
Didn't you hear? (*Moves toward Ines. Pause*) How can I go to
sleep? Why go to sleep, when I feel like shouting! (*Laughs*)

(*Pepe touches Ines's face. She smiles and kisses his hand. Julio
turns in the other direction. Ines lies back on the raft. Pepe
admires her beauty. The sound of a large wave. The lights change.*)

Scene 5

*"Fifth Day Out at Sea" is projected on the screen. Nighttime. Fog. The
men are asleep. Ines is awake looking into the distance. She is hallucinating. The sound of a large ship approaching.*

INES: Julio, Pepe . . . Are you awake? (*Pause*) I'm going to get ready,
you hear. They're out there. They've come for us. You two
can stay here sleeping, I'll come back for you . . . Where's
my shawl? (*Starts looking for her shawl*) What did I do with
my shawl? I bought it years ago. I'm going to wear it when
we get there. I'm going to run through the seaport with my
shawl. Julio, Pepe, can you just see me! You both have to
carry me in your arms and lift me up in the air.

Best to put some powder on. I probably look like a scare-
crow. Don't want those people on the ship to see all these
long nights on my face . . .

(*She takes out her compact and starts powdering her face hur-
riedly. The sound of a large ship approaching.*)

Eyes red . . . lips dry . . . Lucky for this . . . couldn't leave it
behind, same compact Mamá used for years . . . just in case
I had to see her face in the mirror . . . Oh, if she could peek

from the sky and see that I'm finally getting somewhere! She used to say, "Ines has butterflies in her head." Well, you could tell her now: "I'm going to some big land, Mamá!" They've come for us! . . . And when you have to go, you have to go . . . Even if I had to leave like a thief, without my traveling shoes, my old blue dress, which I hung in my wardrobe years ago, and my alligator bag . . .

—You both have to hold tight to me when I come back for you. Don't want you falling behind. *(Continues powdering her face)* Morning comes and it's all the same here . . . The two of you should've been awake a moment ago—an angel came from heaven and said he was going find us a lightbulb to light this part of the sea. You have to light it when he gives it to you. It would make things better, you hear me. That way I can look for your light in the distance.

(She closes her compact. She has powdered her face so much that it is stark white; she looks like a clown.)

I'm just going to make my way to that ship—to that man waving at me. Good-bye, Julio. Good-bye, Pepe . . . you just keep your eye on my umbrella, you hear me?

(She turns upstage and opens the umbrella. A blue glow emanates from it.)

Just keep your eye on my umbrella, so you can see me in the distance.

(She sticks her foot in the water. The lights slowly start to dim.)

Water is warm, Julio, like a glass of warm milk . . . You liked to drink warm milk at night. They say it soothes the mind, like summer rain. Oh, I can feel the warmth rising to my face.

(The sound of an approaching ship will echo till the end of the scene.)

That's a good omen. It's warm like a winter coat, as if a fallen star had bathed in it . . . Look at all this blue water, Julio . . . nothing like the sea . . . nothing like the sea . . .

(Her voice echoes. The sound of foghorns.)

All these different blues . . . Prussian blue, Pompeii blue . . . aquamarine . . . aniline . . . indigo . . .

(The lights are now completely dimmed. All we see are the light from the kerosene lamp on the raft and the glow of the blue umbrella as it moves farther and farther upstage, away from the boat.)

Calamine blue . . . Capri blue . . . Egyptian blue . . . You just keep your eye on my umbrella, you hear me? . . .

(Then the umbrella is gone.)

JULIO *(Waking up)*: Ines . . .

(Pause.)

Ines? Pepe, wake up! Where is Ines? *(Lifts the kerosene lamp)* Where did she go?

(Pause.)

Ines? Ines . . . Where did she go? Where is she?

(The sound of a large ship fills the stage. The lights change.)

Scene 6

AIRE

"Aire" is projected on the screen. Daytime. Both men are still in a hallucinatory state, looking out into the distance.

PEPE: Nowhere to be found. She's . . .

JULIO: No. Don't say she's gone. She's not gone. She's not gone. Look to your right. She's bound to appear. *(Picks up the compass, tries to get a direction, then throws it)* Oh, this shit!

PEPE: Julio, you've lost your mind. She's gone . . .

JULIO: No. Don't say she's gone. When it's quiet like this . . . when it's quiet I can hear her.

PEPE: Me, too.

JULIO: Then don't say she's gone.

PEPE: No, I hear her, too. But I think it's a ghost . . . Then you start screaming at me, and we lose her. We see her then we lose her.

JULIO: I won't yell at you anymore. When it's quiet like this . . . Do you hear now?

PEPE: No.

JULIO: When it's quiet . . . I can hear her so clear.

PEPE: Then it's real. Then she's really with us . . .

JULIO: You think so, too?

PEPE: Sure.

JULIO: Then it's her.

PEPE: It's a ghost, Julio.

JULIO: No.

PEPE: Then we have to tell ourselves that we're not seeing things—that it's really her.

JULIO: Yes . . . yes . . .

(Ines enters, holding her umbrella, singing a song like "Veinte Años." She makes her way to the raft and sits by Julio.)

Ines . . .

INES: Shshhhhh . . . You see the blue calamine waves over on that side . . . that takes us to a sleepy island where I like to go for tea in the afternoons.

JULIO *(To Pepe)*: It's her . . . *(To Ines)* It's you . . . I told him . . .

INES: Shshhh . . . Not too loud . . . a woman told me that if I stay here for too long, someone is liable to recognize me . . .

JULIO: No. Stay. We won't say anything . . . we won't tell.

PEPE: No we won't tell.

INES: She said, "You go on. You just go on . . ."

JULIO: She said that! That's good . . . We . . . we're glad . . .

PEPE: We thought . . . we thought you had gone . . .

JULIO: Don't say it, Pepe . . . She's here now . . .

INES: Well I said, "I need to get out of this limbo . . . What about Julio and Pepe?"

JULIO: You said that?

INES: The woman told me I could sit here and wait for the ship with you . . . *(Laughs)* I said to her it's easier for others to do this . . . It's easier for a real person, for a man to do these things, because he can hide his face under a hat . . . I'm not supposed to be here. Someone could recognize me. She said she would get me a red scarf . . . *(Becomes excited)* Can you believe it, me sitting here with you wearing a red scarf? And I said, "Could I possibly be dreaming this?" I mean, if I'm not . . . if I'm not . . .

JULIO *(Looks at Pepe)*: No, it's real. It's real like my skin and bones . . . You . . . you . . . you're here . . .

PEPE: Sure, it's real . . .

JULIO: As long as you don't go anywhere . . . and you stay here with us . . .

INES: Of course, my love . . . Someone said there's a bus that comes around this time . . . we don't want to miss it . . .

JULIO *(Going along with her)*: No, we don't want to miss it.

PEPE: But tell them not to send us any ugly phantoms, like last time . . . the ones that took you away . . .

JULIO: Pepe, that's enough!

PEPE: They did. They came here on a black bicycle ... they came here and drank all our water and ... and ...

JULIO: It's all right. This morning I was making my bed before I got up, because I had already gotten up in my mind and made the bed ... And I made the bed because we had things to do. We had to look for you, my love ...

PEPE: Where's the northeast current? That's what we're looking for ...

INES: You must follow the North Star, if you want to find the northeast current. But who can trust stars, I've noticed they're like dizzy sailors, who faint and fall into the sea.

JULIO: Then how do we find our way through this mess?

INES: By the blue trains of the sea ... the constant trains crossing the sea ...

(The sound of a distant train.)

JULIO: I never heard of a train crossing the sea. You mean ... you mean the currents?

INES: There are trains of water sailing everywhere ...

(The sound of the train is getting louder, the train is getting closer.)

Can you hear them? I must go! I must go! The trains ... The trains ... *(Gets up to go)* I'll try to come back! I'll come back!

(The sound of the train gets louder.)

JULIO: Wait ... wait ... Don't go ... you can't go ...

(The sound of the train fades. Silence.)

INES: Soon ... very soon ... Any minute now trees and flowers will surround you again. I know so ... I must go now.

PEPE: The water ... the water ... it's getting shallow around here, Julio ...

INES *(Starts looking for her shawl)*: Oh Julio, where's my shawl? What did I do with my shawl ... I'm going to get to wear it when we get there ... I'm going to run through the seaport with my shawl ...

(Julio helps her look for the shawl. He finds a cloth bag.)

JULIO: Could it be here? What's in here? *(Hands her the bag)*

INES *(Opens it and pulls out the pillowcases)*: I brought those. Didn't want to leave them behind. Take one for you and one for you, Pepe ...

PEPE: What is this for?

INES: I invented this game ... Put it over your head, Julio ... Show Pepe, how to do it ...

(Julio takes a pillowcase and puts it over his head. Pepe lets Ines cover his head as well. She looks at the two of them, then looks into the distance.)

Soon it will be over. Look at our night almost coming to an end, just like everything else ... That's what I'll miss Julio, seeing the morning get dressed before my eyes—how she pulls her clothes from the sea ... Well, what can I do? I move on. That's one thing I learned from the sea ...

JULIO: Ines ...

INES: Yes ... I move on, Julio ... When you lift up the pillowcase, you'll begin a new life ...

(Music plays. She opens her umbrella and walks away. She disappears. Both men remain with their faces covered. The white screen lifts to reveal a green landscape. The men uncover their faces. Blackout.)

END OF PLAY

LORCA
IN A
GREEN
DRESS

Production History

Lorca in a Green Dress premiered on July 12, 2003, at Oregon Shakespeare Festival (Libby Appel, Artistic Director; Paul E. Nicholson, Executive Director) in Ashland, Oregon. It was directed by Penny Metropulos; the set design was by William Bloodgood, the costume design was by Deborah M. Dryden, the lighting design was by Michael Chybowski, the sound design was by Jeremy E. Lee; the dramaturg was Douglas Langworthy and the stage manager was D. Christian Bolender. The cast was as follows:

LORCA WITH BLOOD	Armando Durán
LORCA IN BICYCLE PANTS	Juan Rivera LeBron
LORCA AS A WOMAN	Heather Robison
LORCA IN A WHITE SUIT	Jonathan Haugen
LORCA IN A GREEN DRESS	Christofer Jean
GUARD	Terri McMahon
GENERAL	Ray Porter
FLAMENCO DANCER	La Conja

Characters

LORCA WITH BLOOD, a man in his late thirties

CHORUS:

LORCA IN BICYCLE PANTS, a man in his twenties

LORCA AS A WOMAN, a woman in her forties

LORCA IN A WHITE SUIT, a man in his late thirties

LORCA IN A GREEN DRESS, a man in his late thirties

GUARD, a woman in her thirties

GENERAL, a man in his forties or fifties

FLAMENCO DANCER, a woman

Note: The Chorus members play multiple roles as indicated in the script.

Time and Place

A place called the Lorca Room in a sort of Purgatorio (a room of the soul). 1936.

Author's Note

I took the liberty of using some of Lorca's language in the play, because I felt it was important to hear some of his actual words. Some of the lines I used were modified to fit the dialogue and rhythm of the characters. The dialogue set in italics is taken from Lorca's writing: *Collected Poems: Federico García Lorca* (Revised Bilingual Edition) by Federico García Lorca, edited by Christopher Maurer, Farrar, Straus and Giroux, New York, 2002; *Prosa* by Federico García Lorca, Alianza Editorial, Madrid, 1969.

Qué silencio de trenes bocaarriba!

(The silence of derailed trains!)

—Federico García Lorca
"Nocturno del Hueco," *Poet in New York*

ACT ONE

Darkness. Voices only.

GUARD AS A FASCIST *(Reading names from a list)*:
Miguel Fernández Benavides (Socialist)
Ernesto Baroja (Independent)
Manuel Castillo Delgado (Socialist)
Juan Contreras Espinosa (Anarchist)
Agustín Gímenez Gil (Republican Leftist)
Federico García Lorca (Poet).

(The lights come up, revealing the Guard and the General.)

GENERAL AS A FASCIST: Poet?
GUARD AS A FASCIST: That's correct, General.
GENERAL AS A FASCIST: Who wrote this?
GUARD AS A FASCIST: I did, General.
GENERAL AS A FASCIST: You wrote "poet"?

GUARD AS A FASCIST: That's correct, General. That's what he told me every time I asked him.

GENERAL AS A FASCIST: Go get el hijo de puta.

GUARD AS A FASCIST: He's not here, General. *(Pause)* They've already taken him.

(The lights reveal Lorca with Blood lying on the floor.)

LORCA WITH BLOOD: Who's there? Who's there?

(The lights reveal the Chorus.)

LORCA IN BICYCLE PANTS: *Your life now a legend.*

LORCA AS A WOMAN: *The train that derailed.*

LORCA IN A WHITE SUIT: *The silence of your absence.*

LORCA IN A GREEN DRESS: *The shadow of your face. The dream of who you were.*

(The loud sound of the City of the Dead closing its doors.)

LORCA WITH BLOOD *(Agitated)*: What was that sound? Don't let them gag me! Don't let them gag me!

(Another loud sound.)

L. GREEN DRESS *(Throwing Lorca with Blood a green glove)*: Here, to stop the little stream of blood.

LORCA WITH BLOOD: *Oh, it's just a slash on the cheek.* Nothing more.

L. WHITE SUIT: Nothing more? You're full of blood.

LORCA WITH BLOOD: *I just want to sleep.*

L. BICYCLE PANTS: *The sleep of apples?*

L. WOMAN: *The sleep of the child who wanted to cut his heart out.*

(Another loud sound.)

LORCA WITH BLOOD (*Looks around, wants to know where the sound is coming from*): What is that sound? Where is it coming from?

L. WHITE SUIT: Just the doors closing.

LORCA WITH BLOOD: The doors? What is this place? Who are you?

L. WOMAN: The higher agents of your being.

LORCA WITH BLOOD: You mean . . . (*Laughs*) I think . . . There's been a mistake . . .

CHORUS: No.

L. WHITE SUIT: No. There hasn't been a mistake.

LORCA WITH BLOOD: Yes, of course. Pardon me . . . Maybe you don't know who I am. I was just thrown in here. I haven't even introduced myself. I am Federico García Lorca. I am a poet. And may I ask who you are?

L. WOMAN: I am Federico García Lorca. And he is . . .

L. BICYCLE PANTS: I am Federico García Lorca.

L. WHITE SUIT: I am Federico García Lorca.

L. GREEN DRESS: I am Federico García Lorca.

(*The Flamenco Dancer steps forward and begins taconeo [footwork].*)

CHORUS: She's Federico García Lorca.

LORCA WITH BLOOD: Caramba . . . (*Brings his hand to his eyebrows*) I didn't know . . . I didn't know there were so many of me. (*Laughs; then playfully*) Well, who's the real Federico then? Will the real Federico step forward?

(*All of them take a step forward.*)

I see. (*Laughs*) I ought to step forward, too, no? It's like a little dance, isn't it?

(*Just as he is about to take a step, he notices blood on his shirt. Then, desperately:*)

I'm full of blood. I'm sorry. I've . . . It's just . . . My apologies . . . Please, all of a sudden I feel . . . I have forgotten . . . I must be somewhere . . . (*Runs across the stage, trying to make out his surroundings, then he returns*) Please, tell me what is this place? Who brought me here?

L. GREEN DRESS: The gypsies did.

LORCA WITH BLOOD: The gypsies?

L. WOMAN: They brought you on a green horse, in a green wind.

LORCA WITH BLOOD: And where are they now?

L. WHITE SUIT: They left on a green horse, in a green wind, and left behind a green wave of dust.

LORCA WITH BLOOD: Is there any way . . . ? Please, is it possible . . . ? Call them back! There's been a mistake. I'm only wounded, you see.

Let them know that I haven't died. A wall of bad dreams separates me from the dead.

It's all a dream . . . Look at me, *the grass recognizes my steps, my breath* . . . Look . . .

It was all a dream. Call them back!

L. BICYCLE PANTS: We can't call them back.

LORCA WITH BLOOD: Then I ought to be running along. I know my way back. I know Granada like the palm of my hand.

GUARD: You're not in Granada.

LORCA WITH BLOOD: Then where am I?

GUARD: The Lorca Room.

LORCA WITH BLOOD: The Lorca Room?

L. WOMAN: Like the Vermeer Room, the Goya Room . . .

LORCA WITH BLOOD (*Laughs*): Ah, you should've told me, like a museum.

L. WOMAN: Well, if you want to use those terms.

GENERAL: Remind him of his death.

(*A screeching sound.*)

GUARD: Versions of your death.

L. WHITE SUIT: Versions of your death—One:

> (*The Flamenco Dancer begins a driving rhythm of palmas [hand clapping used for rhythm during Flamenco dancing]. The Chorus enacts the death scene. Lorca in a White Suit plays the prisoner.*)

GUARD: Everything is prepared.

GENERAL: The prisoner is being escorted by two guards.

GUARD: There is blood on your face and in your hands. You are shoved into a truck.

GENERAL: The key to the ignition is turned, and the truck begins to move.

GUARD: A few kilometers away from Granada, the truck comes to a stop.

GENERAL: You are asked to walk six meters from the vehicle.

GUARD: The truck lights shine on you.

GENERAL: You try to say something.

> (*Blinding lights on Lorca in a White Suit.*)

L. WHITE SUIT: Guards!

GENERAL: Shut up, maricón, or instead of shooting I'll finish you off with a knife.

GUARD: A gunshot!

> (*The Flamenco Dancer stamps her feet. The rhythm of her steps creates the sound of gunshots. Lorca in a White Suit falls to his knees. Then he gets up again. The Flamenco Dancer resumes her palmas.*)

L. WHITE SUIT: Guards, understand that by taking a person's life . . . !

GENERAL: Shut up, you faggot!

GUARD: A second shot!

> (*The Flamenco Dancer stamps her feet, then continues clapping. Lorca in a White Suit falls to the ground. The General walks toward Lorca in a White Suit and aims the gun at his buttocks and shoots.*)

Third shot!

> (*The Flamenco Dancer stamps her feet.*)

LORCA WITH BLOOD: I want out! I want out!

> (*Lorca with Blood starts running, trying to find a way to escape. Lorca in a Green Dress runs after him. Lorca with Blood discovers that there is no exit.*)

L. GREEN DRESS: There is no way out, Federico. There is no way out.

LORCA WITH BLOOD: Why are you doing this? Why are you playing with my mind? Are there no angels here?

L. GREEN DRESS: Angels?

L. WHITE SUIT: Angels fly over men's heads, not here.

LORCA WITH BLOOD: So, what kind of place is this?

GUARD: You'll be in this room for forty days.

LORCA WITH BLOOD: Forty days? Quarantine?

GUARD: Quarantine, my dear poet.

LORCA WITH BLOOD: Are you treating me like an animal, or do you suspect that I am carrying an infectious disease?

L. WHITE SUIT AND L. WOMAN: Nothing of the sort.

L. WOMAN: The gypsies brought you here and we're following their instructions.

L. WHITE SUIT: After a person dies . . .

LORCA WITH BLOOD: Señor, be a little more discrete, I'm not dead. I'm only wounded . . .

(Laughter from the Chorus.)

L. WHITE SUIT: According to some gypsy and Islamic beliefs, after a person dies, he is given a dream body for forty days.

L. GREEN DRESS: With a dream body you can wander about and meditate on your life.

LORCA WITH BLOOD: This is a dream body! You call this a dream body—with blood on my shirt!

GUARD *(To Lorca in a Green Dress)*: Give him your green dress.

(Lorca in a Green Dress starts to undress. He remains in a pair of trousers and an undershirt. Hypnotizing piano music plays.)

LORCA WITH BLOOD: What is that music? I remember that music.

(The Flamenco Dancer begins to sing a soft cante hondo.)

L. GREEN DRESS: When you were a little boy, you used to spend hours looking at yourself in the mirror trying on your mother's combs and mantillas. You'd lean over and kiss your reflection on the mirror and whisper little words, "Why didn't you come to my window last night, my love."

(Lorca in a Green Dress slips his dress on Lorca with Blood. Lorca as a Woman, now as Mother, assists him.)

LORCA WITH BLOOD *(Lost in a memory)*: How do you know these things?

L. GREEN DRESS *(Moves close to and touches his face)*: The exact time you said, "I dreamed of kissing your eyebrows and hands through the balustrades."

(Lorca in a Green Dress kisses Lorca with Blood on the lips.)

LORCA WITH BLOOD *(Laughs. Shakes his head as he comes out of his stupor)*: The more I listen to you the more I think Dalí is behind all this. Where is he? Tell him to come out. For a moment I was falling for it.

(In a loud voice) Dalí, come out! It's magnificent!

(To the Chorus) The whole room is surreal. He had told me about these kinds of rooms and inside he would install a surreal world. A paranoiac reality.

He's done this for me, hasn't he? (Walks to another part of the room) He told me that in the future there would be museums in the desert where artists could re-create worlds.

(Applauds) It's magnificent, Dalí. You've created a stage . . . Bravo . . . bravo . . . Come out . . . Let me see you and hug you . . .

GENERAL: Remind him of his death.

(The loud sound of the City of the Dead closing its doors.)

GUARD: Versions of your death:
L. GREEN DRESS: Versions of your death—Two:

(The Flamenco Dancer begins a pulsing palmas. The Chorus enacts the death scene. Lorca in a Green Dress plays the prisoner.)

CHORUS: The truck stopped on the side of a road. The poet walked in front of the truck. His back facing the truck lights.
GUARD: There was no moon.
L. WHITE SUIT: The poet walked in a straight line. He turned around and said something.
L. BICYCLE PANTS: No, a white light came out of his mouth.
CHORUS: A gunshot!

(The Flamenco Dancer stamps her feet.)

A second gunshot!

(The Flamenco Dancer stamps her feet.)

Another gunshot!

(The Flamenco Dancer stamps her feet.)

GENERAL: Is everything a little bit clearer now, Señor Poeta? Let's go over some symptoms you'll experience after death. One: Momentary relapses of life are to be expected.

GUARD: A: You will feel a rush of blood. B: You will see mirages or experience optical illusions. C:

L. BICYCLE PANTS: You will feel unbearable urges.

GENERAL: Two: Ghost pains are to be expected.

GUARD: A: You will feel pain where the bullets pierced your body. B:

L. WHITE SUIT: You might even have the sensation of bleeding.

GENERAL: In time you will learn to recognize these symptoms as figments of your imagination.

L. GREEN DRESS: You will get used to walking without a shadow.

L. WOMAN: You will have the sensation of having a gray coat wrapped around your shoulders and that would only be the weight of your light gone dark.

LORCA WITH BLOOD: Stop it! You're worse than the slithering worms and the green flies that surround death. Get me out of this thing! Mierda! *(Tears off the dress)* You're worse than a pack of rabid dogs gnawing at my flesh. *(Runs)* How do I get out of here? Get me out of this place!

(Lorca in a Green Dress picks up the dress from the floor.)

GUARD: We told you there's no way out.

LORCA WITH BLOOD: I know where I am now. I know who you are. You're here to torment me. You're . . . you're the same guards . . . The ones . . . the ones who spat on my face . . . the ones who wanted to crush my head and pull out my brains. I know who you are. The ones who asked questions. The ones who wanted to get inside me. Haven't you hurt me enough? What do you want from me! What do you want!

L. WOMAN: We don't want anything from you, Federico.

GENERAL *(Calmly)*: The task behind the Lorca Room is for you to come to terms with your perished existence, so you can ascend to another level. Here we have classified moments of your life, and archived them into specific categories, but not before each moment is examined carefully with the microscopic eyes and keen sensibility of our experts. Here in the Lorca Room we have restored some of your memories. There are moments in life in which recollections start to wither. Memories no longer can reveal what they have witnessed and they start to vanish. In your case we've been able to identify three types of memories. The first kind tends to fade like photographs; it seeps inwards as if it wants to bury itself in a void. Who wants to play the part of the poet in a memory?

(Lorca in Bicycle Pants raises his hand.)

L. GREEN DRESS: I do.

GENERAL: Then let's give him an example.

L. WHITE SUIT: I'll play Rafael, your lover, Federico.

GENERAL *(In a loud voice)*: Roll memory.

(Sepia light. The Chorus enacts the memory.)

GUARD: Rolling memory. Take one.

L. BICYCLE PANTS: There you are in Granada after the opening of your play *Yerma*, next to you is Rafael Rodriguez Rapún, your love. You've been drinking wine.

(Lorca in a Green Dress plays Lorca in Granada. Lorca in a White Suit plays Rapún.)

L. GREEN DRESS *(As Federico)*: I want to get away from the Theatre and reporters. Let's go to Cádiz for a few days, just the two of us. Let's spend a few days together close to the sea.

L. WHITE SUIT *(As Rapún)*: That's not possible . . . not now.

L. GREEN DRESS *(As Federico)*: But we're free. The show is a success.

L. WHITE SUIT *(As Rapún)*: My father questioned me about you. He asked about certain rumors he's heard.

L. GREEN DRESS *(As Federico)*: What rumors?

L. WHITE SUIT *(As Rapún)*: I had to tell him that you love women, that everything else they say about you comes from evil tongues. I assured him that it was all a lie.

L. GREEN DRESS *(As Federico)*: It never stops, does it? I feel like running to the top of the hill and shouting out to the world!

L. WHITE SUIT *(As Rapún)*: Then you will never stop shouting.

L. GREEN DRESS *(As Federico)*: I have never stopped even in my silence.

GENERAL: End memory!

GUARD: End memory!

GENERAL: The second type of memory is the kind that stays full of color, when you're young and full of life.

Who wants to play the part of the poet?

(Lorca in Bicycle Pants raises his hand.)

L. GREEN DRESS: I will.

GENERAL: Who wants to play the parts of the painter Salvador Dalí and his sister?

L. WHITE SUIT: I will.

L. WOMAN: I'll play Dalí's sister.

GENERAL: Then let's begin. Roll memory.

GUARD: Rolling memory.

GENERAL: There's the painter Salvador Dalí sitting next to you, facing the sea.

GUARD: There is Ana María Dalí with a parasol.

(Federico is laughing hysterically. Dalí is trying to make a point about his artistic vision.)

L. GREEN DRESS *(As Federico)*: You're mad.

L. WHITE SUIT *(As Dalí)*: Close your eyes.

L. GREEN DRESS *(As Federico)*: No. You're mad.

L. WHITE SUIT *(As Dalí)*: Do as I say.

L. GREEN DRESS *(As Federico)*: Fine. *(Covers his eyes)*

(Dalí shows Federico a sketch.)

L. WHITE SUIT *(As Dalí)*: Now open your eyes and look at the sketch. See how the image gradually disappears, how it changes into another image.

L. GREEN DRESS *(As Federico)*: Incredible!

L. WHITE SUIT *(As Dalí)*: Hallucinogenic!

L. GREEN DRESS *(As Federico)*: Yes.

L. WHITE SUIT *(As Dalí)*: A paranoiac reality! This is what I'm after. The transcription of reveries. Ana María, stand there. Look at Ana María by the edge of the sea. Imagine an open doorway on her back, and through that doorway you see the sea. Or imagine a portrait of her face and close to her eyebrows without any anatomical modification another image, a thousand snails.

L. WOMAN *(As Ana María)*: Why do they have to be snails?

L. WHITE SUIT *(As Dalí)*: Because they have to be snails.

L. WOMAN *(As Ana María)*: Why not a thousand rose petals?

L. WHITE SUIT *(As Dalí)*: And why not a thousand worms? A whole paranoiac delirium. Images on top of other images, layers of details as if seen through a mirage, a languid and melting dream.

L. GREEN DRESS *(As Federico)*: Then poems ought to be written this way. And lovers should love in the same way.

L. WOMAN *(As Ana María)*: Are you saying that lovers should melt into one?

L. GREEN DRESS *(As Federico)*: Yes. And we should be able to love in an infinite continuum. On the first layer of skin of the beloved we should find a sea of moons. On the second skin a forest of trees and a fish swimming. We should love and see art the same way we see dreams, like a continuous road without intersections or end.

L. WOMAN *(As Ana María)*: So the beloved becomes more than a body.

L. GREEN DRESS *(As Federico)*: More than a beating heart . . .

L. WHITE SUIT *(As Dalí)*: Sensory phenomena. Then all reality dies in love as it does in a dream.

(Ana María and Federico applaud.)

L. GREEN DRESS *(As Federico)*: Bravo!

L. WHITE SUIT *(As Dalí)*: Well, I don't want all the applause, but I do. Gracias, gracias. And my dear sister, and friend Federico, we have just seduced reality and the world is surreal!

L. GREEN DRESS *(As Federico)*: Ah, yes, I'm in love with a chair!

L. WOMAN *(As Ana María)*: And I'm in love with my parasol!

L. WHITE SUIT *(As Dalí)*: And I'm in love with a black telephone! We are all seduced by a surreal paranoia.

L. WOMAN *(As Ana María)*: Ah, love, surreal!

L. GREEN DRESS *(As Federico)*: In that case let's have this ant be a priest and let's have a wedding.

(They all laugh hysterically.)

GENERAL: End memory!
    This is the life that was taken away from you, Federico. The third type of memory . . .

LORCA WITH BLOOD: No. I don't want to know!

(A bell rings.)

GUARD: Recess. Take ten minutes.

(The Chorus moves toward the audience. They sit in empty chairs and stretch. Lorca with Blood remains onstage, alone.)

L. GREEN DRESS: Finally, my feet hurt. Joder! That's the problem with Spanish shoes, they're hard, as if they were made from bull hide.

Granadino, how is it going?

LORCA WITH BLOOD: I have no clue. I'm in a quandary.

L. GREEN DRESS: It's always like this. You'll get accustomed to it after a few days. As they say back in Spain: "A lot more was lost when we lost Cuba."

LORCA WITH BLOOD: I just want to know when the torture will stop.

L. GREEN DRESS: Torture? Listen to you! When a baby is born, the child must cry as a sign of accepting existence. If the baby doesn't cry, you have to give him a little spank to see if he has accepted reality. It's the same here. You have to wake up from the dream of life.

LORCA WITH BLOOD: Don't take me for a fool. I know I'm not dreaming.

L. GREEN DRESS: Then when are you going to learn that not dying is not the same as being alive?

LORCA WITH BLOOD: If all of this is true, why don't I remember who closed my eyes? Why don't I remember who leaned over me to hear the silence of my heart?

Or did someone forget to close my eyes? There's nothing worse than a dead man with open eyes. No, mustn't think of these things.

(He closes his eyes as if praying.)

Because death breeds death, I must keep account of what's being taken from me.

Because death means submission and acceptance, I mustn't lose judgment.

Because death is exact, I mustn't lose precision.

Because death is mischievous, I mustn't trust the moon playing hopscotch . . .

(Looks upward) La vida . . . La vida . . . *(Opens his arms)* I'm still alive.

This is a dream. It's all a dream. I've entered a play. This is a play. I am writing about death like before and I've entered the writing.

Life is shouting with illusions and words, and that's what it is. I have to think of the world when I was full of life, there by the sea. By the shore of the sea with Dalí and Ana María.

(Finding confidence) —And you, boy, with the bicycle pants! You look young. What do you do with your time here?

L. BICYCLE PANTS: I work. I'm in charge of the files that have to do with your childhood. I'm in charge of the files that have to do with your dreams.

LORCA WITH BLOOD: My dreams.

L. BICYCLE PANTS: Yes. I place your dreams in vellum papers like butterflies.

LORCA WITH BLOOD: And how did you get a hold of my dreams?

L. BICYCLE PANTS: A man on a green horse was in charge of delivering them every morning, just before dawn. We have photographic negatives of all your dreams. We have drawers full.

LORCA WITH BLOOD: How come you are responsible for my dreams?

L. BICYCLE PANTS: Because you dreamed the most when you were a boy.

LORCA WITH BLOOD: And what else do you do with your time?

L. BICYCLE PANTS: Oh, I have my hands full. You have enough dreams to keep a person busy for a thousand years.

LORCA WITH BLOOD: And do you ever feel the desire to run away from here?

L. BICYCLE PANTS: I do.

LORCA WITH BLOOD: And what do you do when that happens?

L. BICYCLE PANTS: I sit and watch one of your dreams. —The one where your family is having a picnic. Your mother and your brother, Francisco, are eating a little black moon. Your father is smoking a cigar, enjoying the crepuscular light. Your sister is playing with a doll. And you are running with a white balloon around the green olive trees.

LORCA WITH BLOOD: That's enough! It's like watching a bird fly with torn wings.

L. BICYCLE PANTS: What happened, señor? Those were good dreams.

LORCA WITH BLOOD: They were, like green apples and grass.

And in this place? . . . Is there a way of entering the realm of dreams? Can I enter my mother's dreams or my father's?

L. BICYCLE PANTS: It's possible. That's usually done when the dreamer who is part of the world requests it. And the dreamer has to pray. Oh, it's a long process. It involves long periods of vigil and supplications.

LORCA WITH BLOOD: What about the opposite? Must the dreamer always make a request? Can I request to be an apparition in a dreamer's orbit?

L. BICYCLE PANTS: There have been cases in which special permissions have been granted. And these have been issued to the departed souls that have had accidental deaths and wanted to communicate with the world of the living.

LORCA WITH BLOOD: And how can I do it? How can you help me?

L. BICYCLE PANTS: You would have to fill out a requisition, and it takes a few days, sometimes more than a week.

LORCA WITH BLOOD: And can you speed up the process?

L. BICYCLE PANTS: You haven't even accepted your own death.

LORCA WITH BLOOD (*Abruptly*): No!

L. BICYCLE PANTS: Lower your voice.

LORCA WITH BLOOD: I'm sorry . . . My mind . . . (*Laughs sadly*) Sometimes I go in and out of reality. I forget this is a dream and I have to speak softly.

L. BICYCLE PANTS: What do you mean?

LORCA WITH BLOOD (*Grabs him by the elbow desperately*): Please, I feel as if I have gone through an explosion . . .

Listen to me . . . There are things I must communicate while I still have time. While I have some blood left in me.

L. BICYCLE PANTS: Let go.

LORCA WITH BLOOD: I know you can help me. Can you do this for me? Through one of these dreams, can you help me communicate with the world?

(A bell rings.)

L. BICYCLE PANTS: Recess is over.

LORCA WITH BLOOD: Please!

L. BICYCLE PANTS: Control yourself. We must get back.

(Lorca in Bicycle Pants walks away and joins the rest of the Chorus, now back onstage.)

GENERAL: Resumption.

GUARD: Resumption.

(Lorca with Blood squats down and covers his head as if confused.)

GENERAL: Resumption, Señor Poeta.

LORCA WITH BLOOD: Señores, solo una palabra! One word! You are ridiculing me, and to laugh at a person's life is an aberration. My life is not a puppet play. I'm not a puppet.

GENERAL: It's all what you make of it, Federico. Death plays death in this room, absence plays absence and you must play your part, too.

LORCA WITH BLOOD: And what is my part, may I ask?

GENERAL: What is his part he asks?

(The Chorus laughs.)

We have a problem, cast. The protagonist doesn't know his part.

L. WHITE SUIT: Maybe we should go over the roles we are playing. I'm playing Federico García Lorca in a white suit: the poet, the dramatist, the outspoken politician.

L. WOMAN: I am playing Federico García Lorca as a woman: the muse, all the women in his plays and the voice of the other half of the poet.

L. GREEN DRESS: I play Federico García Lorca in a green dress. I play dark love, the poet's secrets and desire.

L. BICYCLE PANTS: I play Federico García Lorca in bicycle pants: all the dreams and the childhood of the poet.

(The Flamenco Dancer does a sensual, gliding seguidilla step.)

LORCA WITH BLOOD: And she plays?

CHORUS: Federico García Lorca:

L. GREEN DRESS: dark sound,

L. WHITE SUIT: the death-seeking spirit,

CHORUS: el duende.

GENERAL: And we are the impresarios of this company. We run the show. We get to play the producers, the guards, the killers, the extras. All of us play the extras. And guess who you play, Federico?

LORCA WITH BLOOD *(Jokingly)*: The moon.

GENERAL: Oh no! You've played the moon before. Here you play the dead poet. *(In a loud voice)* Political position of the poet.

GUARD: Political position of the poet.

(The Chorus creates a judicial court. Lorca in a White Suit plays the defendant.)

GENERAL: Next.

GUARD: Oh, is it time for me to sing in court? *(Pause)* A little song to remind the poet . . .

GUARD AND CHORUS: . . . why he was killed in the Civil War.

(The Chorus sings a song:)

CHORUS:
>The king who is so renown
>gives up one day the crown.
>How can it be!
>
>The poor battle the rich
>in a nation without king.
>This cannot be!
>
>The liberals take over the land
>and the socialists with their clan.
>How can it be!
>
>They call it the Republic,
>the Communists made it public.
>This cannot be!
>
>So Franco goes uphill
>with his rifle and quadrille.
>How can it be!
>
>They call it war in Spain
>and there's nothing to explain.
>How can it be! How can it be!
>
>The Russians come to fight
>Americans keep their plight.
>This cannot be!
>
>And Lolita at the bar
>drinking bourbons in this war.
>How can it be!

Her red lips are much darker
than the cape of the bullfighter.
This cannot be!

And the Fascists with a boom
leave her pallid like the moon.
How can it be!

So put away your reds
the summer always ends.
How can it be!

They call it war in Spain
and there's nothing to explain.
This cannot be! This cannot be!
Ti ri ti tí, ti ri ti, tí . . . Pin panh!

GUARD: Ay! Every time I hear this song I get goose bumps. Poor
    Lolita, killed for wearing red lipstick during the war.
GENERAL: Who will play Federico García Lorca in court?
L. WHITE SUIT: I will. *(Takes a step forward)*
GUARD: Federico García Lorca do you wear red lipstick like Lolita?
    Are you a Marxist?
L. WHITE SUIT: I'm for the people! Workers, women, shoemakers,
    bakers, children . . . I never belonged to any political party.
GUARD: Objection! Irrelevant!
GENERAL: Objection sustained.
GUARD: Will the court instruct the defendant to answer the
    question!
GENERAL: Answer the question, yes or no.
LORCA WITH BLOOD: I can answer the question.
CHORUS: Oh!
LORCA WITH BLOOD: No, I'm not a communist.
L. WHITE SUIT: Thank you, Federico.

GUARD: I have here that you were invited to the Intellectual Alliance for Cultural Defense. This is an anti-Fascist international organization. The event was a pro-Soviet tribute to Maxim Gorky, who had died two weeks before.

L. WHITE SUIT: I didn't go. I turned down the invitation.

GUARD: Why then at five o'clock when you thought of the event, did you think of Gorky? Then your mind wandered to Chekhov. Why Chekhov?

L. WHITE SUIT: Because whenever I thought of Russia, I thought of Chekhov and not Gorky.

GUARD: Then at 5:01 you forgot about the whole event. But you thought of Rafael Alberti, a Communist; Ricardo Baeza, a Communist; María Teresa León, another Communist. Why?

L. WHITE SUIT: I knew they would be at the event. They had organized the whole thing. They wanted me to join the Communist Party. I knew the event had nothing to do with Gorky. It was all propaganda.

GUARD: Didn't you sign a telegram that was sent to the Russian government?

LORCA WITH BLOOD: I can answer that question. Of course I signed the telegram. A great artist had just died. I wanted to pay my condolences to the Russian people.

GUARD: Objection!

GENERAL: Sustained.

GUARD (*To Lorca with Blood*): You also signed a telegram that the Communist magazine *Socorro Rojo* published on the first of May to all the workers of Spain.

LORCA WITH BLOOD: I'm for the people, señores. But I don't belong to any political party.

GENERAL: Smells like the color of red lipstick to me.

GUARD: And this other magazine? Tell us about *October, Revolutionary Artists and Writers*.

LORCA WITH BLOOD: It was started by Alberti and his wife. They had been to Berlin and had seen what was happening there.

They had seen with their own eyes the burning of the Reichstag. What Hitler was doing in that country. They wanted to denounce all of it. They wanted to alert the people of the evil they had witnessed.

GUARD: So, it's an anti-Fascist magazine.

Your name appears on the list of signatories.

LORCA WITH BLOOD: Well, I was seeing the hundreds of Jews that were arriving in Madrid every day. Every time I went to Madrid to do a play there were more Jewish refugees.

GUARD: So does this further explain your photo in the Communist paper?

LORCA WITH BLOOD: I'm not responsible for any photos, señores. I'm not a photographer. The photo was taken of me.

GUARD: But you can take responsibility for the exact place that you were when the photo was taken. *(Produces photo)* Here you are with open arms reciting a poem next to the Brazilian Communist Luis Carlos Prestes, during a solidarity demonstration.

LORCA WITH BLOOD: I recited a poem at the event in support of the workers—the people.

GUARD: Well that certainly makes him red.

GENERAL: The poet died from three gunshots. One bullet pierced his right lung, two bullets pierced the buttock area. As one of the killers said, "We shot him right in the ass, the way you shoot a Communist faggot."

Is your death a little more clear now, my dear poet? Do you accept your present condition?

(Lorca with Blood is silent.)

Silence is good, Federico. That means the bullets hit the right spot.

L. BICYCLE PANTS: Well, a little scene from his childhood to brighten things a bit.

GENERAL: Scenes from his youth. Give him a taste, hombre!

GUARD: Roll scenes from the poet's life.

L. BICYCLE PANTS: Your life as a little boy.

(The Flamenco Dancer begins to sing. Green lights bathe the stage.)

CHORUS:

    Verde que te quiero, verde.

L. BICYCLE PANTS:

    Verde que te quiero verde.
    Green as I would have you be.

L. GREEN DRESS:

    You appear as a child
    given birth to by the moon,
    placed in this green nest of Granada,
    where you drank milk from the fountains of Alhambra
    and the gypsies sang green lullabies.

CHORUS:

    Verde que te quiero verde.
    Green as I would have you be.

L. WOMAN:

    You come bathed in green blood,
    green river water, green air, green light.
    You lie there in wait as though in a green ambush
    until someone whispers your green name, Federico.

GENERAL: Federico.

GUARD: Federico.

L. BICYCLE PANTS:

It's not long before your mother,
the moon,
comes back.

L. WOMAN:

She enters through the window,
like a gypsy thief.

L. GREEN DRESS:

You taste in her milk
a green desire.

L. BICYCLE PANTS:

A yearn for an obscure green,

L. GREEN DRESS:

green eyebrows,

L. WOMAN:

green hands,

L. GREEN DRESS:

a green waist, a green gaze.

L. WOMAN: Ay vida! Que vida! Que verde era tu puta vida!
L. WHITE SUIT: One 5th of June we give you a piano.

(A little piano is presented to Lorca with Blood.)

LORCA WITH BLOOD: I remember the piano. I remember the room
where the piano was placed. The piano was here. And not
far from the piano was a rocking chair, in which my sister
Conchita used to sit and listen to me play. There was a song
I used to sing.

(Lorca with Blood closes his eyes and sings "Canción China en Europa":)

> La señorita del abanico
> va por el puente del fresco río.
>
> La señorita del abanico
> va por el puente del fresco río.

(Lorca with Blood returns to life through the song. His eyes are full of tears.)

GENERAL: Are you missing something?
L. BICYCLE PANTS: He's had enough for today. Let him rest.
L. WOMAN: Let him rest, hombre!
GENERAL: All right. Workday has come to an end.
GUARD: Workday is over.

(A bell rings. Most of the Chorus members walk off.)

LORCA WITH BLOOD: Young man.
L. BICYCLE PANTS: I can't talk right now.
LORCA WITH BLOOD: But the dreams . . .
L. BICYCLE PANTS: Whatever it is, I can't.
LORCA WITH BLOOD: Just tell me if it can be done.
L. BICYCLE PANTS: No. There are risks involved.
LORCA WITH BLOOD: What's the worst that could happen?
L. BICYCLE PANTS: I could lose my points.
LORCA WITH BLOOD: Points? Points for what?
L. BICYCLE PANTS: I got to go. I got to go . . .

(Lorca in Bicycle Pants exits. Lorca with Blood and Lorca in a Green Dress are alone.)

L. GREEN DRESS: What do you want from that boy, Federico?

LORCA WITH BLOOD: Nothing. I was just . . .

L. GREEN DRESS: You can forget about fishing stars from his hair.

LORCA WITH BLOOD: I just want to know more about this place.

L. GREEN DRESS: Is that all you want from that boy?

LORCA WITH BLOOD (*Laughs at his mischievousness*): You . . . You are clever. What do you know about these points he is talking about?

L. GREEN DRESS: Points to move to a higher level. Ascension.

LORCA WITH BLOOD: Does this mean that he is . . . ?

L. GREEN DRESS: Yes.

LORCA WITH BLOOD: Does this mean that all of you are dead?

L. GREEN DRESS: We don't use that word around here. "Retired from life" we use.

LORCA WITH BLOOD: Then how did you . . . ?

L. GREEN DRESS: Retire? The bullet hit me right here. (*Points to his head*)

LORCA WITH BLOOD: I see.

L. GREEN DRESS: The end is a terrible thing. It's placed in our lives from the moment we are born, but we learn not to recognize it.

LORCA WITH BLOOD: And this room?

L. GREEN DRESS: Just see it as a place to organize the life you left behind. It's like a passport office where they fix your papers, so you can get your visa and ascend to another level.

LORCA WITH BLOOD: So it's like Purgatory?

L. GREEN DRESS: No, more civilized, less religious.

LORCA WITH BLOOD: Does this mean that a room is created for every person that has died?

L. GREEN DRESS: Are you kidding! Do you realize how many people are being killed every day in this war?

LORCA WITH BLOOD: And how come I get to have a room?

L. GREEN DRESS: Because the control station recognizes that you are a poet, and all souls are rewarded or corrected as they merit. Poets revive life, my dear. Every time you write, you make us see the world in a new way, so you revive life. That's why you are high on the list. As for people like me who didn't do much in life, I'm number 2,035 on the list. So what can I do! Now I'm an actor working in the Lorca Room, so I can get points and speed up the process. Joder, if I had known this before, I would've put on my skates in life.

LORCA WITH BLOOD: I want you to teach me all the rules of this place. I want to know if there's a way out of here.

L. GREEN DRESS: Well, you'd have to break the quarantine.

LORCA WITH BLOOD: Break the quarantine? Leave before the forty days are up?

L. GREEN DRESS: Sure. As simple as that. *(Laughs)*

But do you want to become a ghost? That's what some do when they can't go along with the rules of this place. They become walking dead men, rude ghosts that walk through walls and enter houses without announcing themselves. If I were able to go back to life, I wouldn't want to be a little wisp of smoke. I'd want to have lots of flesh and black hair, brown eyes and beautiful lips.

(Pulls out a flask and gives it to him) Here, drink. You don't want to be a spook.

LORCA WITH BLOOD: Anything to go back, my friend.

L. GREEN DRESS: Take this. Smell this liquor.

LORCA WITH BLOOD: Can one drink here?

L. GREEN DRESS: No. *(Laughs. Opens the flask)*

LORCA WITH BLOOD: And how . . . ?

L. GREEN DRESS *(Smelling the liquor)*: Easy. The man who delivers the dreams likes me. I do him some favors. I help him remember his wife and he pays me with this.

Here. *(Lorca with Blood is about to take a swig)* Don't imbibe. Just smell the spirits.

LORCA WITH BLOOD *(Brings it to his nose)*: Whiskey?

L. GREEN DRESS: Yes, like expensive perfume.

LORCA WITH BLOOD *(Takes a whiff)*: Strong.

L. GREEN DRESS: Not too much. A little goes a long a way.

LORCA WITH BLOOD: I never thought I'd be inhaling whiskey in Purgatory.

L. GREEN DRESS: Well, I know it wasn't an easy life for you.

LORCA WITH BLOOD: You can say that again.

L. GREEN DRESS: I know it wasn't an easy life for you. *(Laughs)* Many broken nights.

LORCA WITH BLOOD: Broken nights?

L. GREEN DRESS: Yes, men that you loved: Salvador Dalí, Emilio Aladrén and the other one, Rapún. Many nights in which they couldn't touch you as a man.

LORCA WITH BLOOD: I guess there's nowhere to hide in this place. I might as well nail myself to the wall like a painting.

L. GREEN DRESS: I'm sorry.

LORCA WITH BLOOD: Here. *(Gives him the flask)*

L. GREEN DRESS: Forget I said anything.

LORCA WITH BLOOD: I've been humble all my life, but I always felt that I deserved to be loved.

(Silence.)

L. GREEN DRESS: Well, don't get sad. It's all behind you now. Think about the good times. That's what keeps me going. Tell me about the happiest moment in your life?

LORCA WITH BLOOD *(Smiles)*: Being by the seashore with Dalí and his sister. Visiting the two of them in Cadaqués. We'd spend endless hours by the shore of the sea. It was so blue. *(Lost in thought now)* And the two of them made it even bluer.

L. GREEN DRESS: What happened between you and Dalí?

LORCA WITH BLOOD: Why do you ask?

L. GREEN DRESS: Rumor has it . . .

LORCA WITH BLOOD: If he ever came close to me, it was to make love to my mind.

L. GREEN DRESS: Your mind? Your head?

 Well, he is certainly strange. I guess Dalí would do something like that.

 Was the sister anything like him?

LORCA WITH BLOOD: She was pure like water.

 There were moments I could've loved her.

 It would've been so much easier in the world if I could've loved a woman.

L. GREEN DRESS: Ay, the world! The world! It always comes down to the world. Look at it now infested with bullets. It gets worse every day, doesn't it? Will the killings ever stop?

LORCA WITH BLOOD: No. The Fascists have taken over. They want to scalp the soul of the country and nothing will stop them. They enter people's houses in the middle of the night. They take them away without any warning, and if they refuse to go, they kill them in front of their mothers.

L. GREEN DRESS: Puta madre! What did they tell you when you were arrested?

LORCA WITH BLOOD: They said that my pen was worse than poison. They accused me of being a Communist.

L. GREEN DRESS: Weren't you a red?

LORCA WITH BLOOD: No.

L. GREEN DRESS: I was. Red as a lobster. People called me Carmen la Langosta.

 I used to live under a bridge with my mother. I made money dancing. I had a poodle that I trained to dance flamenco. His name was Enrique. He was part of my act.

 When the guards attacked me they killed the poor thing. It took one bang right here with a rifle *(Points to his nose)* and the poor Enrique was gone.

 Every time I think . . . Every time . . .

LORCA WITH BLOOD: Criminals!

L. GREEN DRESS: Bastards that's what!

LORCA WITH BLOOD: How could they kill an innocent creature?

L. GREEN DRESS: They're scum, animals with rifles. They are the faggots, who powder their faces with gunpowder! Rabid dogs. *(Shouting out)* May their hands rot from gangrene!

LORCA WITH BLOOD *(Shouting)*: Their tongues!

L. GREEN DRESS: Their lips . . .

LORCA WITH BLOOD: Their throats . . .

L. GREEN DRESS: May their livers burst with bile! And may the bile enter every part of their body until they can taste their own bitter gulp, and gasp from the same substance that festers their souls. And . . . and may their eyes burst out of their sockets, and may they cry tears of blood!

(From the tirade, they break into a release, and begin to laugh. They can't stop laughing. They laugh even more. The Chorus reenters and watches them. Lorca in a Green Dress joins the Chorus, then they exit.

Lorca with Blood finds himself alone onstage. He looks around the room. He sniffs the flask.)

LORCA WITH BLOOD: Is it a dream? Is it?

(He looks around again to see if there is someone in the room. He takes a swig from the flask. Blackout.)

ACT TWO

The Chorus surrounds Lorca with Blood. They laugh and dance. They are having a blast. Lorca with Blood is singing "Canción de Jinete." He has changed the whole atmosphere of the room. There is joy in the air.

LORCA WITH BLOOD (Singing):
>   En la luna negra de los bandoleros
>   Cantan las espuelas.
>
>   En la luna negra de los bandoleros
>   Cantan las espuelas.
>
>   Ay, caballito negro,
>   Donde llevas tu jinete muerto?
>
>   Donde llevas tu jinete muerto?

(Looks up and cups his hand) Sometimes I still feel life like a handful of wind I've stolen from the world and placed in my pocket. That's when I know that I must go back and return this little pocket of life.

LORCA WITH BLOOD AND CHORUS *(Continue singing)*:
> . . . *Las duras espuelas del bandido inmóvil*
> *que perdió las riendas.*
>
> . . . *Las duras espuelas del bandido inmóvil*
> *que perdió las riendas*
>
> *Ay, caballito frio.*
> *Que perfume de flor de cuchillo!*
> *Que perfume de flor de cuchillo!*

(The Chorus applauds.)

GENERAL *(Stepping out of the Chorus)*: What is going on here? Resumption.

(The music ends.)

GUARD *(Entering)*: Resumption.

(A bell rings.)

GENERAL: What is going on?
GUARD: Reporting the progress of the poet.
GENERAL: Oh, I can see his progressing. And how is he progressing?
GUARD: Not much progress, señor.
L. WHITE SUIT: He goes in and out of reality.
GUARD: Sometimes he thinks he's alive, other times he faces the truth.

GENERAL: That's to be expected.

L. GREEN DRESS: Illusive heart pulse still detected.

L. BICYCLE PANTS: Green fog in his eyes.

GUARD: Green landscape detected in the retina.

GENERAL: Repeat death sequence.

(*The Chorus reenacts the death violently as a way of breaking the Poet.*)

L. WOMAN: Truck stops.

L. WHITE SUIT: Communist!

GUARD: Homosexual!

L. WHITE SUIT: No moon!

GENERAL: Bullet!

L. GREEN DRESS (*As the Poet*): Civil Guards!!!

GENERAL: Bullet!

L. GREEN DRESS (*As the Poet*): Civil Guards!

L. WHITE SUIT: Maricón!

GENERAL: Bullet!

L. WOMAN: No moon.

GENERAL: Well, Federico?

LORCA WITH BLOOD: Your act seems a little repetitive for my taste. And I'm a Spaniard, and all Spaniards have a fondness for death.

GENERAL: Then why don't you write your own end sketch, my dear poet?

(*Laughter from the Chorus.*)

L. WHITE SUIT: That sounds like a brilliant idea. What kind of end would you write?

L. WOMAN: I'd like to play a tragic death.

L. WHITE SUIT: But that's not the way a poet dies.

L. GREEN DRESS: And how does a poet die?

L. WHITE SUIT: A poet should die pricked by a rose thorn.

GUARD: No, a poet should die like this, like this, drowned by words:

> Amanecer. A gasp. Niebla. Another gasp.
> Penumbra. Three gasps.
> Y volar. Adiós. The levity of flight.

L. WHITE SUIT: Now that's poetic! *(Applauds)*

(The entire Chorus applauds.)

GENERAL: Federico, should we give you pen and paper?

LORCA WITH BLOOD: Would the players care to enact a death that doesn't end, but a death that remains? A death that stays alive in people's minds. The kind that won't let the criminals sleep. The type that enters a house and shouts like a child. Death that washes her face in the morning when the killers look in the mirror.

GENERAL: My dear señor, on this particular plane of existence we correct inner conflicts, the wrestling of worldly impulses. We are not interested in carnal justice.

LORCA WITH BLOOD: Then I'm afraid I'll have to break this quarantine you are subjecting me to.

L. WOMAN: Why quit now, Federico? You only have thirty-seven more days left. We will help you get through it. We are sculptors of desire.

At the end of the forty days in this room, you will find yourself in a state of submission, transformed from being desirous to being yourself desired. The consummation of your soul will have the same geometry as the imposing and sublime Alhambra.

L. GREEN DRESS: Don't quit, Federico!

L. BICYCLE PANTS: Take my word, don't do it.

(The General puts his arms around Lorca with Blood's shoulders and takes him around the room.)

GUARD: Take this opportunity and make use of what this place has to offer you.

L. GREEN DRESS: You can visit Buenos Aires again without leaving the Lorca Room.

L. WHITE SUIT: You can visit Havana without having to cross the Atlantic.

GENERAL: How about New York?

LORCA WITH BLOOD: No!

GENERAL: Why not?

GUARD: He never found what he was looking for in New York.

GENERAL: And what was he looking for?

L. GREEN DRESS: He was looking for an escape.

L. WHITE SUIT: Isn't everyone trying to escape something in New York?

LORCA WITH BLOOD: I imagine everyone is trying to escape the cement.

(Laughter from the Chorus.)

GENERAL: And what was the poet escaping from?

LORCA WITH BLOOD: I was trying my luck.

L. WOMAN: He was escaping the embers of two eyes.

LORCA WITH BLOOD: Señores, por favor. It was difficult enough living through it once.

(Soft guitar music begins to play. We hear the sound of a ship's horn.)

GENERAL: Is this the way he embarked the ship to New York?

GUARD: Yes, listless and crippled. With a suitcase of dead love.

GENERAL: Who was the dead love?

(Lorca in a Green Dress opens a suitcase. Out of it, he removes a sculpture of two hands holding a crescent moon.)

L. GREEN DRESS: The sculptor Emilio Aladrén, who did away with the poet's heart.

CHORUS: Ahhhh!

GUARD: And what else was the poet escaping from?

(An image of the moon descends from above.)

L. WOMAN: He was running away from the moon.

CHORUS: Ahhh, la luna!

L. WHITE SUIT: He was escaping the gypsies.

GENERAL: The gypsies! Wait a minute, wasn't he called the "Poet of the Gypsies"?

L. WHITE SUIT: The poet was running away from what Dalí and Buñuel said of his gypsy ballads.

(The Flamenco Dancer enters with a guitar. Lorca in a White Suit cuts the guitar strings with a pair of scissors.)

"Folkloric and stereotypical," they said.

GUARD: What else was he running away from?

L. BICYCLE PANTS: He was running away from his color green.

(Lorca in Bicycle Pants pulls out a little box with a green light inside.)

CHORUS *(As if in ecstasy)*: Ah, verde!

GUARD: And what did he see in the color green?

L. WOMAN: Desire until death.

> His love's voice from before
> when all the roses gushed from his tongue!

CHORUS: Ahhh!

GENERAL: Well that's a lot of things to be running away from. And that's the life you want to go back to?

LORCA WITH BLOOD: Tomorrow I shall break quarantine.

GENERAL: Break quarantine? *(Laughs)* Players, correct me if I'm wrong, but did the poet just say he still wants to leave the room before his forty days are up?

(The Chorus laughs.)

LORCA WITH BLOOD: That's correct. You heard me.

GUARD: Oh, no, no, no! You don't want to do that.

GENERAL: Well, besides being confused, the poet remains in a stubborn condition. Has anybody told the poet what his options are if he returns to life?

L. GREEN DRESS: I have.

GENERAL: Did you give him a summary of what it's like to wander through life as a dead man? A ghost?

LORCA WITH BLOOD: I'm sure I'll do well, compadre.

GENERAL: I'll give you less than three days and you'll be back knocking at our doors.

(The General exits. The Chorus begins to follow.)

L. GREEN DRESS: Farewell, Federico! We'll keep an eye on you from this side. May God be with you!

L. WHITE SUIT: Adiós.

(Lorca with Blood is about to exit.)

L. BICYCLE PANTS: Federico, don't go back. You will feel like a stranger in the world. Even in familiar places you will feel like an outsider. Why not be more patient?

LORCA WITH BLOOD: Does the month of March wait for September? Adiós, amigo, you could've helped me but you didn't.

L. BICYCLE PANTS: Federico, you are a word dreamer. The dreamer dreams the world, and the world dreams him. When Spain began to dream you, someone decided to put a stop to that dream. Federico, understand. It's important that we maintain lines and borders.

LORCA WITH BLOOD: Then you shouldn't be handling dreams. Adiós.

L. BICYCLE PANTS: Adiós.

(Sound of the City of the Dead opening its doors. The Flamenco Dancer walks toward Lorca with Blood. She blindfolds him with a handkerchief. The Chorus reappears and stays at a distance, narrating the journey back to the world.)

CHORUS: On the third day:

(Blindfolded, Lorca with Blood is brought to center stage by the Flamenco Dancer.)

L. WHITE SUIT: You are given a transparent appearance,

GUARD: silent soled shoes,

L. WHITE SUIT: and a passport without a picture to remind you of your perished existence.

L. WOMAN: Your eyes are covered to cross the symmetrical lines that separate the City of the Dead.

L. GREEN DRESS: You are given a guide.

CHORUS: El duende. On the third day the return begins.

(The Flamenco Dancer opens the road to life through the dance.)

GUARD: There you are in a war-torn country amongst the life takers,

L. GREEN DRESS: amongst the bullets,

L. WHITE SUIT: amongst the wreckers,

L. BICYCLE PANTS: the intruders,

L. GREEN DRESS: the excluded,

L. WOMAN: the heartbreakers,

L. BICYCLE PANTS: the heartbroken,

L. GREEN DRESS: the ignorant,

GUARD: the sodomites,

L. GREEN DRESS: the tailor forced to mend a bullet hole.

(The Flamenco Dancer removes the handkerchief from Lorca with Blood's eyes.)

L. BICYCLE PANTS: You reach your street. You examine your emotions for signs of despair at finding yourself in front of your house.

(Lorca's family appears. Lorca with Blood stands at one end of the stage, opposite his family. Lorca in a White Suit plays the Father, Lorca as a Woman plays the Mother, the Guard plays Conchita, and Lorca in Bicycle Pants plays Lorca's brother Paquito.)

In front of your mother.

LORCA WITH BLOOD: Mamá aqui estoy . . .

(The Flamenco Dancer calls out to the Mother through a dance step.)

Mamá . . .

(The Flamenco Dancer repeats her steps.)

Soy yo, Federico . . . Tu hijo . . . Tu hijo . . .

(The Flamenco Dancer continues to interpret Lorca with Blood's words. The Mother doesn't answer.)

Mamá, don't you recognize me? Can't you hear me? Or have you lost your hearing?

(The Mother doesn't respond.)

What did they do to you? Mamá . . . Madre . . .

(To the Flamenco Dancer) Pregúntale . . . You ask her for me . . .

(Turns to the Father. The Flamenco Dancer does the same) Papá . . . Padre . . . It's me Federico . . .

What have they done to Mamá? Who has mixed silence and sand and cemented her voice?

Papá! Padre!

(To the Flamenco Dancer) Ask him if they have done the same to him! Ask him if they have sewn up his mouth, like they did Mamá! Ask him!

(Turns to Conchita. Almost in a whisper) Conchita, my sister! Look into my eyes. Have they made you a citizen of this silence?

(Turns to Paquito) My brother, Paquito, have they done the same to you? Have they circumcised your voice, like the rest?

(Turns to the Father) Papá háblame tu . . . Háblame . . . Háblame . . . Speak to me before they pronounce the death penalty of words. Speak! Speak to me, Mamá . . .

Through your reflection, through your mantilla, through your comb, but talk, talk!!! . . .

Ay, silencio!!! Why is this silence so loud?

(Silence. The family tableau fades.)

(To the Flamenco Dancer) Go. You can go. You can go on . . . I don't need a guide or a cane. I know the way to my own hell.

(Through dance, the Flamenco Dancer tells him that she won't leave him behind.)

Go. I know my way.

(The Flamenco Dancer tells him that she understands his pain.)

You don't have to worry about me, I'll go and sit in places I've known.

L. BICYCLE PANTS: Camina, Federico . . .

L. GREEN DRESS: Camina . . . In your house there is only silence.

L. BICYCLE PANTS: Camina . . . . Go far away, Federico, and don't stop, don't turn . . .

L. GREEN DRESS: Forget the stench of war.

L. BICYCLE PANTS: Don't look at the guards.

LORCA WITH BLOOD: Traitors!

L. BICYCLE PANTS: Don't look at them!

LORCA WITH BLOOD: Faggots!

L. BICYCLE PANTS: Pick your battles, Federico.

L. GREEN DRESS: Don't look at the Fascists!

LORCA WITH BLOOD: "Don't look at the Fascists! Don't look at the Fascists!" I don't look at them. The ones who have colored their cheeks with innocent blood.

L. BICYCLE PANTS: Vamos camina!

L. GREEN DRESS: Remember your words, your art.

L. BICYCLE PANTS: Remember your whole life.

L. GREEN DRESS: Remember what you left behind.

L. BICYCLE PANTS: Remember the Theatre, the applause.

L. GREEN DRESS: Buenos Aires, Madrid, Barcelona, Havana.

L. WHITE SUIT *(As an Emcee)*: Y ahora señoras y señores, Federico García Lorca, en nuestro Buenos Aires.

(The sound of applause.)

LORCA WITH BLOOD: Gracias, gracias . . . Gracias por los aplausos . . .

L. GREEN DRESS *(As a Fan)*: Everybody is talking about you in Buenos Aires.

L. WOMAN *(As a Fan)*: *Blood Wedding* is a hit!

L. BICYCLE PANTS *(As a Fan)*: *Blood Wedding* is a triumph in Buenos Aires.

L. WHITE SUIT *(As an Emcee)*: Federico, you're called to the stage. The audience wants you to come out again.

L. WOMAN *(As a Fan)*: Can we take a picture, Federico?

L. BICYCLE PANTS *(As a Fan)*: *Yerma* is a success in Barcelona, Federico. Congratulations!

LORCA WITH BLOOD: I don't remember such enthusiasm, not even in Buenos Aires.

L. GREEN DRESS *(As a Fan)*: After every act, the audience wants you to come out on the stage.

LORCA WITH BLOOD: Gracias, gracias . . . Muchas gracias . . .

L. WHITE SUIT *(As an Emcee)*: Federico, the audience is calling you back!

L. BICYCLE PANTS *(As a Fan)*: Federico, go up on the stage!

LORCA WITH BLOOD: Gracias, gracias . . .

(The General enters.)

L. WHITE SUIT *(As an Emcee)*: Federico, the audience is calling you back!

GENERAL *(In a loud voice)*: Open the truck's door.

LORCA WITH BLOOD: Gracias, gracias . . .

GENERAL: Let him walk in front of the truck.

LORCA WITH BLOOD: Gracias . . . Gracias a todos . . .

GENERAL: Prepare arms!

LORCA WITH BLOOD: Gracias . . .

GENERAL: Now shoot! Shoot!

(Sound of a gunshot. The sound of applause ends. Lorca with Blood opens his arms and falls to the floor. The Flamenco Dancer sings a cante jondo.)

FLAMENCO DANCER:

> Blanca y pura luz hay en mi canto
> sol, canela y miel hay en mi pecho.
> Blanca y pura luz hay en mi canto
> flor y verde mar en mi quimera.
>
> Que se levante, que se alce
> que me abra lo ojitos de ese sueño.
>
> Blanca y pura luz hay en mi canto
> sol, canela y miel hay en mi pecho.

CHORUS:

> Blanca y pura luz hay en mi canto
> flor y verde mar en mi quimera.

FLAMENCO DANCER:

> Que yo no quiero ya más llantos
> ni más flores ni tampoco ya más rezos.

CHORUS:

> Blanca y pura luz hay en mi canto
> sol, canela y miel en mi quimera.

FLAMENCO DANCER:

> Blanca y pura luz hay en mi canto
> flor y verde mar en mi quimera.

CHORUS:

> Blanca y pura luz hay en mi canto
> sol, canela y miel hay en mi pecho.
> Blanco y pura luz hay en mi canto
> sal y dulce miel en mi quimera.

L. BICYCLE PANTS: Be not weak, Federico!

FLAMENCO DANCER (*Singing*): Que se despierte, ay mi muerte-
cito . . .

L. BICYCLE PANTS: Be not daunted . . . Be brave and courageous . . .

FLAMENCO DANCER (*Singing*): Ayyyhh . . . Que se despierte, de
este maleficio . . .

L. WOMAN: Don't fear light. Open your eyes!

L. WHITE SUIT: Open your eyes. You exist the way your words exist.

L. GREEN DRESS: Open your eyes.

GENERAL: Step by step, memory by memory, and out of the past
emerges a man . . . And what is this man seeing? What is
he seeing?

LORCA WITH BLOOD: Everything and nothing.

GENERAL: Where are you?

LORCA WITH BLOOD: In a dream that awakened me.

GENERAL: Then go moment by moment. Memory by memory.

LORCA WITH BLOOD: I'm feeling weightless.

GENERAL: And before.

LORCA WITH BLOOD: I'm rising from the floor.

GENERAL: And before.

LORCA WITH BLOOD: I feel the pleasure of life leaving me, gushing from one of my sides.

GENERAL: Go further back.

LORCA WITH BLOOD: The sea.

GENERAL: What sea?

LORCA WITH BLOOD: Yes, me by the shore of the sea.

GENERAL: There is no sea in Granada.

LORCA WITH BLOOD: I never saw Granada. I went away from
Granada.

GENERAL: That's impossible.

LORCA WITH BLOOD: In my mind I did.

GENERAL: Where to?

LORCA WITH BLOOD: After all the questions . . . After the inter-
rogations.

GENERAL: What questions?

LORCA WITH BLOOD: "Do you communicate with Russia?" No. I'm not a Communist. "Do you communicate with Russia?" No. I'm not a Communist. "Then what are you?" I'm not a Communist. "Then what are you?"

GENERAL: Where did you go after the interrogation?

LORCA WITH BLOOD: I told you . . . I told you to the shore of the sea with Dalí and his sister . . .

GENERAL: That's not possible . . .

LORCA WITH BLOOD: It was . . . It was in my mind, when my life was gushing out.

GENERAL: What happened after the interrogation?

LORCA WITH BLOOD: I sent a letter to Papá.

GENERAL: What did the letter say?

LORCA WITH BLOOD: It said . . . *(A gulp of death rises to his throat)*

GENERAL: What did it say!

LORCA WITH BLOOD: Dear Papá . . .

GENERAL: Say it.

LORCA WITH BLOOD: Dear Papá, please give the bearer of this letter two thousand pesetas.

GENERAL: Pesetas for what?

LORCA WITH BLOOD: To get me out . . . Bail me out of that hell.

GENERAL: What do you remember of that hell!

LORCA WITH BLOOD: A dog running with my life in its mouth . . .

GENERAL: And what is that called?

LORCA WITH BLOOD: Nothing and everything.

GENERAL: And what is "nothing and everything"? Tell me!

LORCA WITH BLOOD: No. I went to the sea. I thought of what I never got to have . . .

GENERAL: That's not what I'm asking you . . . Name it once and for all . . .

L. BICYCLE PANTS: Let him talk!

GUARD: Let him talk, hombre.

LORCA WITH BLOOD: I remembered Dalí and his sister . . . We were by the shore . . . They were there . . . It was my last image. Dalí and his sister by the shore of the sea.

(The Chorus enacts the memory. By the sea. Lorca in a White Suit plays Dalí. Lorca as a Woman plays Ana María. Lorca in a Green Dress plays Federico.)

L. WHITE SUIT *(As Dalí, from a distance)*: Federico.

L. WOMAN *(As Ana María Dalí, from a distance)*: Federico.

LORCA WITH BLOOD: There I was with my body washed by the sea, my black hair combed back . . . That's what I was taking with me.

LORCA WITH BLOOD AND L. GREEN DRESS *(As Federico)*: Why is it that I feel so happy when I'm around the sea?

L. GREEN DRESS *(As Federico)*: Why do I like being with the two of you so much?

L. WHITE SUIT *(As Dalí)*: Because you're mentally retarded like Ana María and me.

L. GREEN DRESS *(As Federico)*: You fool!

(Federico charges toward Dalí playfully. Dalí runs away, hiding behind Ana María.)

I want to know what you do when I'm not here?

(Ana María and Dalí look at each other. They laugh hysterically.)

L. WOMAN *(As Ana María)*: When you're not here we're bored out of our minds.

L. WHITE SUIT *(As Dalí)*: When you're not here we wake up in the morning without you, we yawn without you, we look out the window without you, we gaze at the morning without you, Ana María combs her hair without you . . .

L. WOMAN *(As Ana María)*: I say to Dalí, "Buenos dias without Federico."

L. WHITE SUIT (*As Dalí*): Papá says, "It's a good day without Federico."

L. WOMAN (*As Ana María*): The maid yells, "I'm serving breakfast without Federico . . ."

L. WHITE SUIT (*As Dalí*): And we run to the dining room without Federico.

L. WOMAN (*As Ana María*): Papá says, "Can you pass me the butter without Federico?" Tieta says, "Can you pass me the bread without Federico?"

L. WHITE SUIT (*As Dalí*): The maid says, "We ought to buy onions without Federico."

L. WOMAN (*As Ana María*): And we finish breakfast without Federico.

L. WHITE SUIT (*As Dalí*): And I think to myself, Another day by the sea without Federico.

L. GREEN DRESS (*As Federico*): One day I want to sit and describe this place in a poem!

LORCA WITH BLOOD AND L. GREEN DRESS (*As Federico*): Why does it feel like I've known you all my life?

(Ana María touches Federico's face.)

L. WOMAN (*As Ana María*): Because when you're here, time stops, the world becomes fixed.

L. WHITE SUIT (*As Dalí, playfully and dramatically*): Oh, cacharrumpín! Without you I'm a lifeless peanut.

L. GREEN DRESS (*As Federico, playfully*): And does this lifeless peanut need me to give him life?

L. WHITE SUIT (*As Dalí*): Oh, please do. Provide me with life.

L. GREEN DRESS (*As Federico*): Let me give you life, you lifeless peanut. *(Blows air in his face)*

L. WHITE SUIT (*As Dalí*): Ah, I have life now. I have ants crawling around me again! Oh, how good it is to have life!

L. WOMAN *(As Ana María)*: Bravo . . . Bravo . . . .Stay and live with
us forever, Federico.

L. GREEN DRESS *(As Federico)*: Me or Señor Peanut?

L. WHITE SUIT *(As Dalí)*: She's talking about Señor Peanut.

L. GREEN DRESS *(As Federico)*: Ah, of course! Everybody has a
crush on Señor Peanut.

L. WHITE SUIT *(As Dalí)*: Ah, look . . . She brought you a starfish,
Federico. You should've gotten him a lobster.

L. WOMAN *(As Ana María)*: Oh, why don't you just die!

L. WHITE SUIT *(As Dalí)*: Are you going to make him starfish soup
for dinner?

L. WOMAN *(As Ana María)*: Yes, starfish soup for him and rice
mixed with nails and razor blades for you. I hate you.

(The memory ends.)

L. GREEN DRESS *(As Federico)*: Ana María, come back . . . Don't pay
attention to him. Ana María . . .

LORCA WITH BLOOD AND L. GREEN DRESS *(As Federico)*: Ana
María, Dalí, Dalí, Ana María, Ana María, Dalí . . .

LORCA WITH BLOOD: Ana María, Ana María, Ana María . . . Dalí,
are you there? Dalí, Dalí, Ana María, Dalí, Dalí, Dalí, Dalí . . .

(Silence.)

Ana María . . . Dalí . . .

(Silence.)

Oh God!

GENERAL: Do you know where you are now?

LORCA WITH BLOOD: Yes.

GENERAL: Where are you?

LORCA WITH BLOOD: I'm no longer a part of the world.

GENERAL: Repeat.

LORCA WITH BLOOD: I'm no longer a part of the world.

GENERAL: One more time!

LORCA WITH BLOOD: I'm no longer a part of the world.

GENERAL: Good. Are you prepared to accept your present existence?

LORCA WITH BLOOD: Yes.

GENERAL: Good. Are you prepared to ascend to another level?

LORCA WITH BLOOD: Yes.

GENERAL: What do you want?

LORCA WITH BLOOD: I want nothing.

GENERAL: What do you want?

LORCA WITH BLOOD: I want nothing. I want nothing.

GENERAL: No desires?

(Silence.)

LORCA WITH BLOOD: Yes.

GENERAL: And what is that?

LORCA WITH BLOOD: The color green.

GENERAL: Clarify. No metaphors in this room.

LORCA WITH BLOOD: It's the color of the beloved.

GENERAL: That's a physical desire.

LORCA WITH BLOOD: No. It has always been the face of God.

GENERAL: Then you are allowed. Any wishes?

LORCA WITH BLOOD: One.

GENERAL: And what is that?

LORCA WITH BLOOD: To enter the landscape of dreams.

GENERAL: Whose dream?

LORCA WITH BLOOD: My mother's and my father's dream, and the dreams of my sisters and my brother. España.

GENERAL: It is granted.

L. BICYCLE PANTS: Close your eyes. To enter the landscape of dreams, we must go through the motions of associations. If I tell you blue, you will tell me sky and so forth. Is that clear?

LORCA WITH BLOOD: Yes.

L. BICYCLE PANTS: España.

LORCA WITH BLOOD: War, rape, blood, death, my birth, my death
. . . my land.

L. BICYCLE PANTS: Granada.

LORCA WITH BLOOD: Black eyebrows, gypsies and my buried moon.

L. BICYCLE PANTS: Mamá.

LORCA WITH BLOOD: Milk, blood, human water: Vicenta Lorca.

L. BICYCLE PANTS: Padre.

LORCA WITH BLOOD: Precision, tree, and human angel: Federico
García Rodriguez.

L. BICYCLE PANTS: Your two sisters.

LORCA WITH BLOOD: Two boxes of heaven.

L. BICYCLE PANTS: Your brother.

LORCA WITH BLOOD: A dove with a horse's heart.

L. BICYCLE PANTS: Be still and listen.
Do you see the faces of those people you've mentioned?

LORCA WITH BLOOD: Yes . . .

L. BICYCLE PANTS: You're entering the vagaries of dreams now.
What do you see?

LORCA WITH BLOOD: Colors, faces, trees, blood.

L. BICYCLE PANTS: Be not distracted. Enter the river.

LORCA WITH BLOOD: I am.

L. BICYCLE PANTS: Here images take the forms of dreams.
What do you see?

LORCA WITH BLOOD: I'm riding a horse of black water.

L. BICYCLE PANTS: And what do you see now?

LORCA WITH BLOOD: I'm still riding a horse of black water.

L. BICYCLE PANTS: Then go.

*(Lorca with Blood stands up. He looks into the distance. Truck
lights shine on him.)*

LORCA WITH BLOOD:
I'm riding a horse of black water.
A few kilometers from Granada,

a truck comes to a stop.
I am asked to walk six meters from the truck.
The truck lights shine on me.
I walk in front of the truck.
I count five moons.
I walk in a straight line and
I remember that the bull has his orbit
and the bullfighter has his
and I must look at death with geometry, with measure,
with the fundamental basis of a bullfight.

A gunshot. Another gunshot. And another. I enter Granada on a horse of black water. And there beyond a night without God I find the killers.

I enter their houses and my horse takes the form of a dog that feeds on their sleep. I'm there next to their pillows, like an actor after the applause, making nests with their wives' hair, because to kill a man is to get to know him in the most intimate way. And every night of their lives the killers must be resigned to undressing the body of the dead and contemplating the infinite little stream of blood; the gush of words that continues to flow from the ink of a green pen.

Señoras y señores, before the night of theatre descends, welcome to my *legend of fountains,* words that moan, the story of *an orange and a lemon,* a dream of thirteen boats, the voices of hammers singing, my microscopic moons. Here comes the grass. Green wind. Green boughs. Let my play begin.

(The stage is illuminated by a million watts of white-green light. The wailing of a woman. Blackout.)

END OF PLAY

CAPRICHO

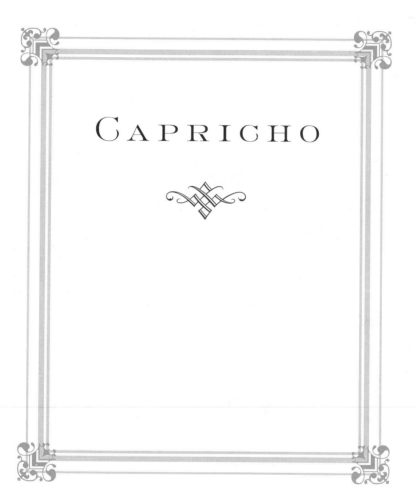

In 2003, *Capricho* was commissioned by the McCarter Theatre Center (Emily Mann, Artistic Director; Jeffrey Woodward, Managing Director) in Princeton, New Jersey, to celebrate the opening of its Berlind Theatre with an evening of short plays: "Berlind Shorts." *Capricho* was directed by Ethan McSweeny and performed by Felix Solis.

A dust of light. A man full of dust. The man, Loló, looks as if he has come out of a Goya painting, but he is actually a forgotten actor in a Lope de Vega play. For years he has been waiting to perform. He is really an understudy. But his mind wanders to other mindscapes and he thinks he is a leading actor. He wears black toreador pants without ornamentation, dark pink stockings, a white shirt and a black jacket. He holds a broom.

Not far from him there is a slumped skeleton. Her name is Manolita. She's also a forgotten actor in a Lope de Vega play. She probably died while waiting to perform. She also looks as if she has come out of a Goya painting. Her early-1800s black dress and large Spanish comb with a black mantilla, were probably inspired by Goya's painting "La Maja." These two characters have been under a trap door for years, but they think they are inside their dressing room.

The dust of light fully reveals Loló and Manolita. We hear the strumming of a guitar and an Andalusian wail.

LOLÓ: Any minute now . . . Any minute now, Manolita . . . Any minute . . . The stage . . . The theatre . . .

(*With excitement*) Ay, madre mía! I have to sweep. (*Starts to sweep*) I have to sweep. I have to sweep . . . I sweep . . . I sweep . . . I know you say I look like a street sweeper. But I have to sweep to keep away the theatre crows. The crows . . . The crows . . . The moths that eat up the costumes, the curtains and those other insects that eat up the stage, the scenery.

(*Turns to the skeleton*) Are you still going over your lines, Manolita? I know you are . . . You don't have to tell me . . . I know how you get before a performance . . . You must be getting nervous already. Not me, that's because I sweep. I sweep before I perform. You have to sweep . . . Sweep like I do. Even if I'm playing King Lear or Laurencio in Lope de Vega's play, I pick up the broom and sweep. Keeps me from shitting on my pants. Keeps the actor in me humble and active.

(*Stops sweeping, he takes a deep breath*) I know you probably want to pee-pee by now. (*Holds his crotch, tightens his legs and bends forward*) Nothing but nerves. That's why I sweep. (*Smiles, sweeps*) Any minute now . . . Any minute, they'll say, "This is your ten-minute call." They'll knock on our door and you best be ready.

(*From the distance we hear knocking on a door and the voice of a Stage Manager. The voice echoes.*)

STAGE MANAGER: This is your ten-minute call. This is your ten-minute call.

LOLÓ: You hear that! Any minute now they'll knock on our door.

How do I look Manolita? (*Fixes his hair, straightens his clothes*) How do I look?

(*Panics*) The props! (*Starts looking for the props all over the stage*)

The props! Where did I put them? Where? Ah, in my pocket . . . In my pocket. The letter . . . The letter . . .

(He searches for the letter in all of his pockets. Then he finds it inside of his jacket pockets. He realizes he is missing another prop.)

My other prop. My other prop . . .

(He looks all over and finds a bouquet of silk flowers under Manolita's dress.)

Ay! You were sitting on top of them! *(Straightens the petals of the flowers)* Look at this. The flowers are dying now!

Get up, Manolita! . . . Get up! You must get ready. Let me fix your dress. *(Stands her up)* They're about to knock on our door and you best be ready . . . Unless . . . unless . . . Well, unless they want to give us the night off as they did last night . . . and the night before that . . . and—when was the last time we got to go on? Let's see . . . *(Counts with his fingers)* Ah, well! It's awfully kind of them to give us so many nights off and have the understudies do the show.

But it takes great effort, enh! It's hard to sit here and listen to them playing our roles. The worst is to hear the one who has my lines. Bah! But he's nothing like me.

(He laughs. He laughs. He keeps on laughing. He fixes his clothes again.)

There can only be one of me. One Loló right, Manolita? Only one Loló, named after a bullfighter. Named by my uncle who was blind and walked with a black dog. *(Laughs)*

(Then, discouraged) But maybe we're not performing tonight. Maybe they forgot to tell us. Maybe they forgot us.

What do you think, Manolita? *(Takes a piece of paper out of his pocket and studies it)* If the schedule hasn't changed . . . No, here it says . . . Maybe they've made a mistake and the other show in rep is on this evening and they forgot to tell us.

(From the distance we hear knocking on a door and the voice of a Stage Manager. The voice echoes.)

STAGE MANAGER: This is your ten-minute call.

(Loló grabs the broom. He hides his nervousness behind the task of sweeping. He is so nervous, he is sweeping and not sweeping at the same time. He is stuck in one place, the broom is a few inches off the ground.)

LOLÓ *(With excitement)*: They're coming, Manolita. They're coming! Any minute now! Any minute!

Oh lord! Oh lord! The potty! The potty! Do you have to go, too? The potty! Do you have to go?

(In haste, he starts unbuttoning his pants. The pants drop. He is looking for the potty but also for the broom.)

No, if I sweep. No, the potty. If I sweep. No the potty . . . I'll sweep! I'll sweep!

(He picks up the broom. He sweeps without sweeping. He is stuck in one spot.)

I know you're feeling it too, Manolita. The excitement. The nerves. This is why we do theatre!

And not going on every night keeps us on our toes. The . . . The . . . The euphoria . . . The . . . the thrill . . .

(Takes a chair and sits her down) Ah, you should've seen me the night I got to go on! The night I got to perform with

María Baranda. That was the beginning. *(Realizing that she doesn't like him to talk about this, he tries to cover it up)* Bah! I know you don't like for me to talk about María. But I say, "The beginning," as one says . . . as one says, "The beginning of the end," hombre, "The beginning . . . The beginning . . ." I say, "The beginning," because there's always a beginning: a clear point of departure when you take your hat and place it on your head to go. And when it's time to go, you go. No one can stop a hat from going, at least not this hat. *(Grabs his hat and puts it on)*

(Panics) Oh lord! What's my first line? What's my first line, Manolita? It's something like . . . If . . . If I . . . If I . . . What's my first line? Ah yes, "If I should . . . If I should . . . If I should find . . . find . . . Shall . . . shall . . . If I shall ever have . . . have . . . If I shall have the likeness of your love, then I shall seek an alphabet of love . . ." *(Savors the lines)* "An alphabet of love!" Ah yes! Love!

(He is transported to another time, a time when he was in love. He stands in his own light.)

Yes. Love. A new alphabet in my mouth. Yes. In every word I'd find her name. In every syllable her hands. Me in love, as if pushed off by God. No longer myself. Threaded to her . . . to her face . . . only her face . . . Ah love!

(He looks at Manolita and realizes that she doesn't like when he wanders off mentally. He tries to cover.)

I'm sorry, Manolita. I wandered off. That was Turín's line. My first line is, "I, my lady . . . I, my lady, dare not . . ." That's my first line. And I say that line to you now, Manolita. I won't dare talk about love in front of you. I know you don't like it when I talk about my past. And before you start pulling out your handkerchief, I promise that I won't talk about María Baranda.

(From the distance we hear knocking on a door and the voice of a Stage Manager. The voice echoes.)

STAGE MANAGER: Actors to the stage. Actors to the stage.

LOLÓ *(In a hushed voice)*: Manolita, they're calling the actors! They didn't call us, but they're calling the actors!

STAGE MANAGER: Actors take places for the top of Act One. Top of Act One.

LOLÓ: Let's just go! *(Takes her by the arm)* Let's go! They forgot to tell us that we're on. We're on. Fix your dress. *(Fixes her dress)*

(From the distance we hear knocking on a door and the voice of a Stage Manager. The voice echoes. Loló and Manolita are frozen, listening.)

STAGE MANAGER: Good evening, señoras and señores! Please take your seats. Take your seats. *Blood Wedding,* by Federico Garcia Lorca is about to begin.

LOLÓ *(In a hushed voice)*: That's not our play. That's not our show. Did you check the schedule, Manolita? *(Takes out the schedule)* Don't take off your costume! Maybe they made a mistake and announced the wrong play. Maybe we'll get to go on. Don't get sad. *(Takes her face in his hands)* We can't afford to get sad.

STAGE MANAGER: Please take your seats. Take your seats.

(Loló sits on the floor. He lies Manolita down next to him. Her head rests on his lap. We hear a beautiful adagio. The music fills the theatre, then starts to fade.)

LOLÓ *(Motionless)*: Listen, the play is starting.

(The lights begin to dim.)

Soon we'll go on. But we must wait. We mustn't be impatient. We must wait with the logic of waiting. With the joy that one waits at a train station for a friend we haven't seen in years. With the dress and the hat you like to wear on Sundays. With the impulse to embrace and kiss this friend once we see him. With our heads full of thoughts and things we are going to tell him. And with the innocence and amazement of seeing things for the first time, like the falling snow.

(He stands her up, leaning her against the wall.)

Let's rehearse! Get up! Let's rehearse! We must wait like this, practicing our honesty and our patience, consenting to play like children. Because when we wait we see things we wouldn't see if we weren't waiting, like the slow season of the dust, and this can only be good for the theatre of life, since we are all meant to play the role of ashes and dust when our time comes. Are you ready?

(A dust of light falls on the two of them. Then everything darkens, as music begins to fill the stage.)

END OF PLAY